I
Ran
Away
With
An
All-Girl
Band

I Ran Away With An All-Girl Band

*My life on the road
with the Victory Sweethearts*

PATRICIA WOLFF

STONE HUT PRESS
Traverse City, Michigan

Publisher's Cataloging-in-Publication
(Provided by Quality Books, Inc.)

Wolff, Patricia (Patricia A.)
    I ran away with an all-girl band : my life on
the road with the Victory Sweethearts / Patricia
Wolff. -- 1st ed.
    p. cm.
    LCCN: 99-91368
    ISBN: 0-9675732-0-3

    1. Wolff, Patricia (Patricia A.) 2. Women
musicians--Biography. 3. Saxophonists--Biography.
4. Victory Sweethearts (Musical group) 5. Big
bands--United States. I. Title.

ML419.W65A3 1999   788.7/165/092
[B]   QBI99-1538

First Edition: November 1999

10 9 8 7 6 5 4 3 2 1

To Freddie and all the girls in the band
for the greatest experience ever.

To our moms
who knew that as women we could go far.

To our sisters and brothers
who were proud of us.

To our children
who have taken up where we left off.

And to Glenn, Paul, and Lisa
who have made me very proud.

Contents

Introduction

I HAVE WANTED TO TELL THIS STORY FOR MANY YEARS. THIS seems like a good time, with all the recent attention given to World War II, the renewed craze for swing dancing, and the sudden interest in my old clothes, which I have never been able to throw away. My grand-daughter has even sewn my husband's old neckties into her blue jeans. Perhaps the wave of nostalgia will be more complete with this story of an all-girl dance band.

Joining a swing band was not something most girls did in the '40s, but we were liberated long before it was the "in" thing. I didn't hes-itate for a second when I was asked to join the band at the age of 14, and never felt held back because I was a woman. I considered myself an accomplished musician, but never much good at improvising, like some of the other girls. We developed into a tight, highly entertaining band, although we were reminded often enough that we "were good for girls." I knew we were just good.

Writing the book was a delight, especially since it brought some unexpected surprises. My younger sister, Sue, recently told me that when the band rehearsed in town, she would sneak in and hide in the shadows and watch us for hours, and then go to her friends and tell them all about her big sister who was with an all-girl dance band. I wasn't able to spend much time with my little sister in those days, but we have made up for it in the years since. I am fortunate to still have both my sisters and my brother to talk to about the good old days.

Researching the book also put me back in touch with some of the old members of the band — Edna, Hilda, and Mackie. Edna, our piano player, who was with the band from the beginning, remembers more about those years than anyone. She even sent me her diary. I call her often on the phone, and we never fail to recall something we haven't thought of in many years. She can still play piano, but her eyesight is failing, so she plays by feel now rather than reading music and writing arrangements like she used to. No matter. Like it has for me, music has always been a big part of her life and will stay that way until the end.

Eventually I sold my saxophone, raised children, and fell in love with the visual arts. My third and last passion in life has been writing. My children — Paul, Glenn, and Lisa — encouraged me all the way, from the first short story I read to them. Their support carried me through on this project, too. Glenn worked tirelessly to help bring this book to print. Paul transferred the tapes of the band's old radio broadcasts to CD, so I could listen to them. Boy, did that bring back memories! Gail Dennis designed the book, capturing the '40s as if she had lived them, and her husband, author Jerry Dennis, who has been my mentor for many years, was a terrific editor. Thanks also go to Anne Stanton, a former editor of mine who has always encouraged my writing, for her generous help with this project. And thanks to Alex Moore for his technical assistance, and to Aimé Merizon for proofreading, and especially my friends in the Grand Traverse Writers Group.

Finally, I want to thank my mom for nudging me mightily into a career in music by arranging private lessons with Freddie Shaffer, the bandleader. Freddie, bless his soul, perhaps deserves the most thanks of all. He taught me how to play saxophone and gave all of us girls a wonderful opportunity.

Those seven years on the road were the best of my life.

Learn the Basics

"OKAY, QUEENIE, YOU'RE ON!" FOR YEARS THAT'S HOW MY husband teased me after I ended my career as a "show girl." I think he was a little jealous. It had to be that. He was a much better musician than I, but he knew that I had had more fun than he. Mine was a life most girls would die for — and most parents would consider a nightmare. That is, if they knew what went on, on the road. I'm still amazed that I played in an all-girl band.

Well, that's not entirely true. My mother made me do it.

Life was pretty normal for most of us teenagers in Frankfort, Indiana. We had our little cliques and our after-school activities and we loved to be noticed by boys. And to make sure they noticed us, we gathered at the drug-store every day after school and often again in the evenings. I always ordered a chocolate coke and slid into a booth with my friends and talked and laughed and talked some more. We were a close-knit group and talked endlessly and effortlessly about everything in our lives. On most of the important subjects — boys, clothes, school, our parents — we were usually in agreement. But when it came to the future, everyone but me seemed to know where they were going and what they were going to do. They all planned to attend college, maybe to get a degree, definitely to get a husband. I asked my friend Sally once what college courses she wanted to take and she said, "sexual inter." Another friend, Phyllis, made no bones about it: She was going to college to get a man. When the war came they married their boyfriends and watched them ship out overseas. But not me. I was different. I wanted to be an entertainer.

My mother was a fairly average parent back in the '30s and '40s in central Indiana. There were four of us kids and though I know now that times were rough, my mother made sure we had all the advantages she had never had, especially a good education. My sister and I took lessons in piano, tap dancing, and elocution, and my little brother learned to play the drums. I could never understand that kid. He insisted he was playing "Old Suzannah" on the drums, when it sounded like the same old racket to us. But Mother encouraged us, even in our clumsiest efforts, and she sewed endlessly to make sure we looked well dressed.

The piano lessons did it. In the end I realized that what I learned on the keyboard made it possible for me to pursue a career in music. It would have never happened otherwise. "If you learn the basics of piano, you can easily learn to play any other instrument." That's what I heard almost every day. But I didn't like piano and I didn't like my teacher, who once broke a ruler across the piano trying to get me to understand tempo. Most of my early teachers had been little old ladies with their hair pulled up in buns, strict but sweet and caring. Not this teacher. She was a large, intimidating, bosomy woman with a boyish haircut who always smelled of cinnamon. With me she had little patience. It was as if she used up her daily quotas of kindness and attention on the young man who had his lesson the hour before mine. He was a wonderful musician, who played with feeling and excitement. I would go early to my lesson just so I could hear the two of them play on the pair of pianos she kept side by side in her studio. They always had a wonderful time playing together. How I wished I could be that good.

Then one day the teacher told her prize student that she had taught him everything she knew and he no longer needed lessons from her. Did this mean I would never hear them play together again? And how could this be — to teach someone everything you know? Was this the way of life? Was it my responsibility to try to learn everything this woman knew about the piano? I carried the burden of this notion with me for what seemed like an eternity and I tried, I really tried, but I didn't seem to get much better. Evening after evening my dad would say, "Patsy, play 'Liebestraume' for me." I never got through it without making a mistake, but he was never critical and he never stopped asking.

It soon was apparent that my teacher had little hope for me. She went through the motions of teaching, but there was none of the enthusiasm she had exhibited with the young man.

I tried a different teacher, a sweet little old lady with her hair up in a bun. But it was useless. I had tired of the piano and wanted to try something different.

"You already know the basics," Mother said, "so now everything else will be easier. What do you want to play next?"

"Clarinet," I said.

In the Beginning

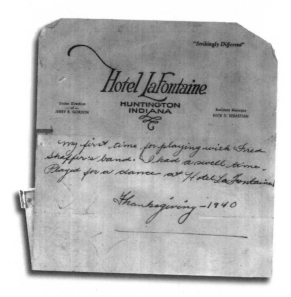

"Strikingly Different"

Hotel LaFontaine

**HUNTINGTON
INDIANA**

Under Direction
— of —
JERRY B. GORDON

Resident Manager
NICK D. SEBASTIAN

my first time for playing with Fred Shaffer's band. I had a swell time. Played for a dance at Hotel LaFontaine

Thanksgiving — 1940

IT WAS A LOT TO ASK. CLARINETS WERE EXPENSIVE, MONEY was short, and teachers were hard to find. So I was surprised my mother agreed so quickly. But it turned out she had lived for this day.

Our neighbor's daughter had recently begun playing in an all-girl band put together by a man named Freddie Shaffer. It was all our neighbor talked about to my mother every day — Margret did this and Margret did that and the band was her life. Mother played every conversation back to us word for word, with a dash of her own envy showing through. She was primed and ready to push me in a new direction.

Freddie Shaffer had played with Paul Whiteman and Fred Waring and other name bands of the era. He quit performing for a time and returned to Frankfort, Indiana, and established himself as a music teacher in the Clinton County schools and in the surrounding counties. But performing must have been in his blood, because in 1938 he brought about fifteen above-average girl musicians together from different school bands and formed a dance band.

My mother was determined that Freddie Shaffer would be my teacher. She called him and asked if he would consider teaching me clarinet. She explained that I had taken piano lessons since I was eight years old, so, of course, I knew the basics. He was interested but wondered if I would consider playing a saxophone instead of a clarinet. His all-girl band — now in rehearsals — needed a saxophone player.

That was all Mother needed to hear. I had my horn the next day. I don't know where the money came from because, as I say, things were rather rough in those days with four kids to raise and my dad working for the railroad. But I was spared any guilt of having to think about my parents' sacrifice. My mother had too much pride for that. And now she could compare my accomplishments with Margret's.

Freddie Shaffer came to our house twice to give lessons. All I recall him showing me were the basic finger positions; what I did with them was left up to me. I played every day, practicing scales and learning popular songs I memorized from the radio. Of course I did not learn as quickly as I wanted and sometimes grew discouraged that I would ever be good enough to join Freddie's band. But I kept practicing and gradually developed a decent sound. One day Freddie called and asked the question I'd been longing to hear: Did I want to start rehearsing with the band?

Rehearsals of Freddie Shaffer's All-Girl Band were held in the back of the Kraft Music Store, a long-established business that catered mostly to area schools. That first evening I was overwhelmed by the endless rows of display cases and the shelves filled to overflowing with everything musical you could ever imagine. Even in the after-hours light the brass instruments glistened like gold and the keys so familiar to my young fingers were as bright as precious drops of pearl.

And then there were Freddie and the girls. Freddie was dressed in casual slacks and shirt, but there was nothing casual about the way he stood before everyone, clearly in charge, while the girl musicians sat in chairs in their various sections — brass, reeds, rhythm. At first I stood to the side, nervous and uncomfortable, unsure of what to do or where to go until Freddie nodded at me and pointed — all businesslike — to a chair in the reed section.

The back room, a storage room, had been cleared on one side, giving us plenty of space to set up. I was so nervous and excited that I couldn't think clearly. Whenever someone spoke to me the words went right over my head. Freddie handed out music for the first piece and when I tried to read it I forgot everything I had ever learned and made horrible sounds that seemed to have nothing to do with music. I was terrible. But then, the rest of the band wasn't much better.

Freddie was patient and good-humored about it all. He made a few teasing remarks and the tension eased. There was one girl in the band who could play anything. This was Edna. She had already written arrangements meant to simplify the music so that we would find it easier to read and, hopefully, we would sound better. At first Edna wrote all of our arrangements. Later we would graduate to old Jack Mason stock arrangements, but Edna's simple formula preceded that by some time and was perfect for inexperienced musicians.

We rehearsed regularly after that. And somehow we got jobs. The Elks, Demolay, our Union Hall, some country clubs and other bookings. We were teenaged girls, inexperienced and naive, yet to my amazement people would come to our performances and stand before us enthralled. We seemed incapable of doing wrong. One night Jack Teagarden came to hear us. I don't remember why he was in the area, though he might have been playing a stage show at the Indiana Roof in Indianapolis or perhaps in Indiana Beach, where a lot of big bands played in those days. I was still too young to go to those places, though of course I knew them by reputation. They were big-time venues for Indiana, and I couldn't imagine more glamorous places to perform.

Little did I suspect that our band would soon be playing at the Indiana Roof.

Jack Teagarden. For years I'd been in the habit of sneaking downstairs after my parents were asleep and sitting in front of our big old radio. I would listen for hours to the famous big bands of the day, broadcasting from the Hotel Astor, the Lincoln Hotel, Roseland Ballroom, the Steel Pier, Glen Island Casino — all places from cities in the East that sounded incredibly glamorous to me. So the name Jack Teagarden really meant something. It was unbelievable to me that this famous musician, whom I admired so much, not only listened to our performance but seemed to enjoy it. He and Freddie retired to a corner of the Union Hall and talked. Although I have no idea what was said, Jack Teagarden would soon help get our band booked by MCA, the Music Corporation of America, one of the big booking agencies of the day. We were already members of the local musicians union, but it was the MCA booking that made our future secure.

The first job I played was at the Hotel La Fontaine on Thanksgiving Day, 1940. I know the date because I wrote it on a piece of hotel stationery. My mother wanted me to look nice and decided my old coat just would not do. She called Mr. Friedman after his department store had closed for the day and asked if he would meet her there so she could have the coat that was in layaway for me. He was happy to do it. People did things like that in those days. Mother probably took him a piece of cake now and then. She often took cake or pie to her neighbors and favorite clerks.

I had never been in a hotel before, had never eaten out in a nice dining room, so I was a little intimidated by the waiters who were being so polite and ready to take my order. I remember ordering something very extravagant, something I had never heard of and very different from what the rest of the band was ordering — lobster newburg, maybe. Freddie had asked us to take it easy on the food — eat a sandwich or something simple and cheap. But I was too dazzled to be frugal. I ignored his request.

The whole experience — the hotel, the fancy restaurant, the stage where we would perform — left me overwhelmed. When we went on stage I sat in my place feeling dizzy. I saw Freddie's lips moving but didn't know what he was saying. When we got hopelessly lost, Freddie, Edna, and Mack would carry the rest of us through. It was a relief to know that no matter what happened, the music never stopped. After the gig was over, while people came up and complimented us on our performance, I knew that I had to work much harder to truly earn such praise. We were a pretty quiet group on the trip back home.

At first all the money that we made went for clothes and equipment. Freddie bought formal gowns that made us look pretty and professional. We got more bookings after the La Fontaine show. Apparently our youthful, clean-cut, midwestern look combined with our musical ability made us fascinating to our audience. A band like ours had never been seen before. Certainly not in central Indiana.

The Early Days

I WAS FOURTEEN YEARS OLD WHEN I PLAYED THAT FIRST GIG. I wouldn't believe it now without that old piece of hotel notepaper written with the message "My first job" and the date. I still had a lot of high school to finish, but I was thrilled to see my future as a professional musician so nicely mapped out for me.

Not everyone was as thrilled as I. The band director at school got upset with me for changing from tenor sax to alto because Freddie asked me to. I remained in the marching band. It was fun to march at the football games, even when we had to get up at dawn to practice before school started. During good weather we practiced at the football field. Other days our practices were held in the gym.

I loved my life. Marching and playing at the games made me feel important, and playing in Freddie's band was like a dream come true. Even at home, there was music. We didn't have money for extras in those years, yet somehow we always found a way to pay for the things we loved — and, of course, music was a thing we loved dearly, so there was a good radio, and there were records. My dad said once that my mother had Midas's knack of turning junk into gold, and he meant the way she wove magic in our house. Mother always made sure that our friends were welcome at almost any time. She baked cookies every day, I think. One night a week we all went to the bakery for fresh-baked sweet rolls. Around the house we played records, my friend James played the piano, my brother pounded his drums, my sister played trumpet, I played my saxophone, and we ate sweet rolls during the break. It was a lively and very, very musical household.

Freddie's band was not playing a lot yet but there was one gig I'll never forget. It was 1941 and we were booked to play a radio broadcast from a photo studio in Frankfort, to be beamed over WKMO in Kokomo, Indiana. We played our theme song, "Moonglow," as we were introduced, then took a break while Mayor Lockwood of Frankfort delivered a speech. Suddenly people backstage began running frantically around the studio. Freddie got the band playing and ordered us to pay attention to our music and not look around. After our performance we learned that the mayor had suffered a heart attack. He died later at the hospital.

We were devastated. Mayor Lockwood had cared deeply about kids and had won our affection by opening a dance hall called the Areo Inn out by our little airport. It had inside and outside dance floors and a huge jukebox that played for free. The cover charge was a dime and Cokes were a nickel and smoking and drinking were forbidden. Our parents took turns driving carloads of kids to weekend dances at the Inn. Some of us girls would make our own dresses for these special nights. My mother made mine, and they all looked like they were cut from the same pattern. There was a style then — very plain short sleeves, a long waist and a band sewn on to accentuate the slim waist lines and flared skirt. It was a great style if you were slim and liked your dresses skin tight.

Mayor Lockwood never made any money on his inn, but he did something for teenagers that should have gone down in history. He was one man who made a difference.

By 1942 the band had settled into the form it would maintain for the next three or four years. Our original vocalist, Janet, had left to enter nurse's training, and now the vocals were performed by Hilda, tenor sax, and Arthella, trumpet. Hilda, who was my roommate, was a natural performer. She was cute and had a sparkle about her. She sang mostly up-tempo songs and could sing anything, though Freddie always chose the songs we performed. Arthella didn't start out as a singer and was more or less cultivated by Freddie. She was in a sort of "teacher's pet" position. (Well, a little more than that, actually, though I didn't know it at the time. All I knew was she sang well and she was pretty.)

When I first joined the band we had a bass player but she quit and was not replaced. So we had a bass but nobody to play it. By then the sheer repetition of playing night after night had polished our sound, and nobody missed the bass player. Then one day Freddie got us a gig that specifically stipulated a bass player, so we had no choice but to find one. Except none were available. Somebody had the idea of tying the strings down on the bass and having one of us stand on stage with it and pretend to play. I was elected. All evening I stood with the bass against my shoulder and my hands on the neck, smiling and making sure I moved with the right beat. I was sure anyone could see that I was a fake, but nobody seemed to notice and after a while I almost convinced myself that I was playing the thing. Apparently I wasn't the only one convinced. After we finished, some man who might have had too many drinks came up to the stage and said I had a nice touch on the bass.

About that time a dynamite drummer and exceptional showman named Mack joined the band and made us even better. Her spectacular drum solos always brought the house down. Mack had a fiery temper; the problem was that she had a speech impediment and when people didn't understand her, she became impatient with them. Sometimes some jerk would think she was kidding and say something stupid and that would set her off. I couldn't blame her — that is until one night when she lost her temper and threw a drumstick and missed her target and hit me instead. I stood up and faced her and told her never to do that again. She cooled down and everything was fine after that.

Looking back at the old pictures and news clips and listening to our old tapes, I can, all these years later, follow our progress — day by day, week after week. We worked hard and did a good job, I still think. It was an incredible life for young farm girls from Indiana and in a lot of ways we were very successful. But I got lonely on the road and tried quitting twice in those seven years. Once, I got a job at an electrical appliance store as a bookkeeper, though I didn't know anything about bookkeeping. All I learned there was the difference between a male and a female plug. I thought that was amusing, but not amusing enough to keep the job. I went back to the band. The second time Hilda quit with me. We went to work making pants pockets at the Levi Strauss plant in Frankfort, a mindless job that threatened to kill us with boredom. Most of our coworkers were Amish ladies with whom we had little in common. On break Hilda and I wanted desperately to smoke cigarettes but were afraid of offending the righteous Amish women. I lasted two days and Hilda lasted two and a half. I called Freddie again and told him that I missed being in the band and begged him to let me come back. I felt bad that I didn't wait for Hilda. But not *that* bad.

On the Road

UNTIL I WENT ON THE ROAD WITH THE BAND I IMAGINED such a life existed only in the movies. And now to be on my own and making a living at music was a fantasy come true.

But it quickly became my job as well as my life. We were required to do the same thing every night, never showing any sign that we might be getting tired or bored, putting our best face forward with every performance. We were women in a man's world and were reminded of it often by men who told us we were unique and played "really good for a bunch of women." How many times did we hear that? It made us nervous wrecks when male musicians came by to check us out. If they complimented us at all, it was always a little half-hearted. The people who seemed to appreciate us the most were the different acts with whom we shared the bill. If the audiences responded to them with applause and cheers, they in turn praised us, which was very nice.

But the men musicians we met were thoughtful in other ways. In those days drug problems existed, but all we knew about them was what we heard in whispers. Yes, we occasionally read about bands getting busted for possessing pot — but only famous bands were involved. It was never an issue with people we knew. But I remember one night we met some guys from another band and they asked a few of us to join them at their hotel to listen to their records. We thought nothing of it and accepted their invitation. Everything seemed okay, even when one guy pulled out some funny little cigarettes and offered them around. I declined because at the time I didn't smoke and thought he was offering cigarettes. But his band buddies told him to knock it off, that we were ladies and didn't do that kind of thing. Then I sort of got the message and thought it was nice to be protected like that. The guys in the other band might also have been thinking that we were jail-bait teenagers rather than young ladies. Anyway, I appreciated the stand they took.

We traveled in style in two big black Buick Roadmasters equipped with jump seats, plus a "Woody" station wagon. The station wagon carried all our instruments and some luggage. We were each allowed one suitcase. The Buicks carried all of us and whatever would fit in the trunks. One of the trumpet players, Phyllis, and our drummer always drove the wagon. Freddie drove one Buick, and Lois (saxophone) drove the other. Traveling went very smoothly.

In those early days, Freddie paid for everything. We each got a salary, of course, but it was more like an allowance. And Freddie made the decisions. One of our major gripes was Freddie's choice of diners. We always knew that if he drove into the business district of a town, he was looking for a diner, usually on a side street. Every town had at least one and they were all the same — converted dining cars that were the era's equivalent of fast-food restaurants. Some had booths and others had only stools and counters where you ate as quickly as possible so the guy breathing down your back from behind could take your place and have his meal. The food was cheap and bland and it came fast. For entertainment you watched the cook frying everything right in front of you.

I remember we once stopped at a diner way out in the country somewhere. I don't know how Freddie found this one. It was late and we caught the owners unprepared. They were nearly out of food and had no help at all except one woman. So we offered to pitch in. We jumped over the counter and went to work and threw together a pretty good meal. Afterward we helped clean up the mess, then Freddie paid the check and we moved on. That was one old diner that we always remembered fondly.

Dorothy Durgin's
Central Artists Bureau
220 E. JEFFERSON STREET
FORT WAYNE, INDIANA

Presents . . . .

Freddie Shaffer All-Girl Orchestra

Resort Life

WHEN I WENT ON THE ROAD I KNEW VERY LITTLE ABOUT LAKE resorts except that they were places where people had second homes to escape the heat of the city in the summer. I had been to Battleground, a church camp in Indiana, but it wasn't on a lake and wasn't exactly a place where people came to bask in the sun. It had a swimming pool, at least — a concrete thing about 12 x 12. You had to use a ladder to climb in and since the water was so damned cold, the ladder got you back out and on the ground pretty fast. This was definitely not a resort. But at the time I liked it, and I hadn't even found religion yet.

Our first resort gig in the summer of '41 was on a lake in rural Indiana. When we pulled into it I thought it looked like the church camp I had gone to summers as a kid, except that it had the luxury of a nice lake. Our oversize transportation, the black Buick Roadmasters, seemed out of character as we pulled in front of the rustic lodge where we would be living. Freddie assigned us roommates and rooms and we unpacked the cars except for the Woody. That was driven to the band shell later so we could unload our instruments.

Hilda was my roommate and I don't think she liked the idea very much. We were all very young but I was definitely the youngest-acting, and that summer I went a little wild with the freedom of being away from my parents for the first time. The heady independence of it combined with my inexperience and irresponsibility maybe made me less than the ideal roommate. The girls cooked meals when necessary, but I never helped because I simply didn't know how. Mother had never made it a priority for her daughters to spend time in the kitchen and I had never bothered to learn to cook. Everyone must have thought I was unteachable, because I was never asked to pitch in. I remember one night several of the girls made chocolate pudding and it somehow turned into ammunition in a pudding fight in the lake — clothes and all. I thought it was hilarious (though my mother would have punished me for wasting food like that). Poor Hilda was disgusted.

So much for fun and games. Freddie started us rehearsing the first thing next morning. Already I was learning what it takes to make a good dance band: practice and repetition. We set up on a bandstand at one end of a large open-air dance floor across the grounds from the lodge. It had old-fashioned trailer-park lights strung around the edge of the dance floor, giving it that summer-resort feeling. We rehearsed every day and played every night. I was still painfully "green" about what was expected of us, and the resort experience was strange and new to me — as it was to most of the girls. I knew what a good band was supposed to sound like — those nights at home listening to the radio had cultivated a deep love of the music — but it was difficult and at times humiliating to make music ourselves. Gradually, however, the routine of rehearsing every day and playing every night paid off. We began starting and ending each tune together. You can't imagine what a revelation it was to suddenly know that we were getting better, and that we were beginning to understand what was expected of a dance band. Early on, the worst part was having guys make remarks about us not being very good, but when things improved, those same guys started hitting on us. That was a step up, I suppose, but it presented another problem. I had never had a guy approach and want to meet me. At home I hadn't even been allowed to date. The first time it happened I was flattered and probably said something stupid because the girls took me aside and warned me not to talk so much and to never give a guy my real name. This advice made no sense to me but I accepted it because I knew the other girls were more experienced in the game. They wanted me to be more businesslike, to act like a lady and keep close to the others in the band, especially when men were around. It got easier to conform and to work harder because the results were so positive. By the time this gig ended we knew a little more about handling men and, more importantly, were sounding like a real dance band.

•••

Lake resorts are usually the best places to work — at least from a musician's point of view. But Buckeye Lake was an exception.

I don't know why it was called Buckeye Lake because I never saw the lake. The only water open to us was a swimming pool about the size for swimming laps. I'm sure there was a lake somewhere but it must have been in a more exclusive area where the summer people lived. Those people didn't frequent the amusement park except at night when they would come to the dance hall. Then it was more often their kids who came to dance.

If it had been my choice, I wouldn't have been there at all. Every night we played against the music of the merry-go-round. That um-pah music drove us mad. We could hardly hear our own beat and the music of that contraption was all in the same key, which was another distraction. The merry-go-round would go non-stop until about 11:00 every night and then for that last hour we could finally play good, relaxed, danceable music. But the place was crowded regardless. Maybe it's something they got used to during the years. Or maybe the general public was tone deaf.

As our salaries became regular, and Freddie started issuing pay slips, he stopped picking up the meal tabs. This wasn't good news to me, as Hilda and I were running true to form. We came to Buckeye Lake almost broke — the result, I'm sure, of poor planning during our shopping sprees. A five-dollar advance from Freddie was not unheard of, but we were too proud to ask for it, so we went instead to the resort market and bought a jar of cheese spread, a loaf of bread, and milk. That was what we lived on for two days before we could draw another paycheck. I suspect the other girls knew but didn't say anything when we didn't show up at the restaurant at night for dinner. We were in our room pretending to enjoy our poverty.

There was another band at the resort. All guys, of course. Whenever we talked to them all they wanted to do was brag about their many successful gigs. Never once did they comment on our music or come to see us play, though we drew more people than they did. It seemed they consciously avoided us, but it might have been because money was just as scarce for them as it was for us. At the time we even wondered if they got paid less than we did. I remember once when we were hanging around the pool one of the guys showed up — this was rare; they usually stayed away — and we had a brief conversation. His part of it went like this: "I think I'll go back to the cabin and knock out an arrangement." That didn't strike us as a good pick-up line. Could it be that we intimidated those guys as much as they intimidated us?

Calumet City, Illinois

THE FIRST TIME I SAW CALUMET CITY I THOUGHT IT LOOKED like something left over from prohibition, complete with gangsters, gambling, bootlegging, and those forty-some bars on the main street. And we seemed to fit right in when we pulled into town in our two big black Buicks with the jump seats and our Woody. It was easy to imagine that the cars carried the "molls," and the wagon was the vehicle of choice for hauling the heavy equipment — the guns and ammo. When I think about this place, it seems like the setting for a B movie.

We had booked into Calumet City because Freddie was told that an agent from Chicago wanted to hear our band and it was a convenient place to rendezvous. We wanted to meet the challenge with grace and dignity, and tried harder than ever to put on a good show.

The stage was small and set behind and above the bar. It wasn't meant for a thirteen-piece band. To make room for the sax section up front, we had to build a riser for the drums, which put our drummer, Mack, almost into the ceiling.

The club catered to a rowdy bunch who were accustomed to shows every night by scantily clad girls who would go out into the audience and sit with the men between performances. When we opened with our soft theme song, "Moonglow," the men looked at us as if to say, "What? This is entertainment?" Arthella came down from the brass section to sing and approached the microphone smiling but looking above the crowd, never making eye contact with anyone. Her performance was so professional that no one would have guessed how vulnerable she felt up there.

Freddie, as usual, was very good at reading the crowd. He quickly realized we needed to do a lot of feature stuff. Mack and her drum solos were the show stopper. She had power and rhythm and was a great hit with this crowd. Arthella and Hilda both sang. For a special feature, another trumpet player joined them in vocals and formed a trio. Freddie then filled in on trumpet. This three-part vocal harmony was a new, exciting sound for us and we were rather proud of ourselves. It played well with the crowd, but still the men of Calumet City made it clear with their coarse laughter and crude remarks that they would be more impressed if we would take our clothes off.

The club was run by an older lady who insisted on inspecting every performer before she went on stage. She was especially careful to check her regular girls to make sure they didn't uncover too much. If they did, she whipped out her needle and thread and sewed a piece of fabric over the exposed areas. No one messed with her. Of course, with us she had nothing to worry about. In our long formals we looked like prom queens.

Unlike the scantily-dressed girls who were paid to mingle with the customers, at intermissions we were always ushered off the stage to a back room. If we wanted to step outside, a guard went with us. If we wanted something to eat, a guard went with us. It was scary and exciting. Mackie, who had replaced me as bass player — and who could actually play the instrument — had her own self-appointed protector, a man who chose to be her guardian angel. He never let her out of his sight at the club. She didn't think this was necessary, but it made us suspect that this place was worse than we might have first thought. Maybe we simply looked more out of place than anyone had a right to in Calumet City.

I had never been to a place where I thought my life could be in danger if I didn't obey the rules — until now. Even the hotel we stayed at in nearby Hammond, Indiana, was rather seedy. Our cars were vandalized even though they were parked under streetlights in front of the hotel (the better to see you with, my dear). This was one gig my parents never heard about; I have recently talked to three of the girls who were there and we all agree that it was the most intimidating place we had ever been. All of this for an audience who wanted only to see skin, and an agent who never showed up.

My Summer of '42
Geneva-on-the-Lake

GENEVA-ON-THE-LAKE IN THE '40s WAS A POPULAR RESORT
town in Ohio, on the shore of Lake Erie. The main street was lined with
small shops and restaurants that catered to the beach crowd or anyone
just visiting for the day. Some of the restaurants were not much more
than a counter where you could walk up and order a basket of shrimp or
a slice of pizza to eat while you strolled along the street. There was a
wonderful bakery that I frequented almost every day because of their
cream-filled chocolate eclairs. Next door was a gift shop that displayed
lots of silver jewelry and clever pieces made from all kinds of shells. I still
have a silver ring set with abalone shell that I bought there.

I don't know what most of the summer homes were like at
Geneva because they were along the shore and out of view from the main
street. The rich kids spent most of the day driving their cars up and down
Main. At night they went to the bars or the dance hall. I noticed one girl

I thought was probably very rich because she wore a wrist watch with dia-monds all around its face. Once, I overheard her telling girlfriends that her grandmother had given her the watch. My own grandmother never owned a watch, but she once gave me a hand-painted plate shaped like a fish. I've always treasured that.

Our home for the summer was The Farm House, which was the remnant of an actual farm that had existed before the resort was devel-oped. It looked strangely out of place, as if it were waiting for the wreck-ing ball and bulldozer to level it to make room for more development. There probably had been a barn and outbuildings at one time, but they were gone now and the house stood alone in the middle of a vacant plot of land.

The inside of The Farm House was as plain as the outside. It was obviously kept only for the help to sleep in. From the front door you entered a big living room with a couch and an old table on the opposite wall. That was about it for furniture. A bathroom on the right was like one we had when my family lived in an old house in Indiana. It was equipped with an antique claw-foot bathtub of the sort that, years later, my children would see for the first time and call a boat. In the back of the house was a large bedroom with three double beds, where six of us slept. It was just a bare room with two windows that faced the back of the prop-erty — not much of a view but it didn't matter since we only slept and washed out our undies there. We kept a clothesline strung across one end of the room.

The other girls slept in single or double beds, with two or three to a room. Phyliss and Mack were always together in a room of their own. It was just understood that they would always be together. At the time I didn't have a clue as to why two women would be so committed to each other. It didn't matter to us. We were more concerned with the series of affairs that Freddie, who was married, had with first one girl then anoth-er. I couldn't understand why any young girl would want to be with such an old man. After all, he was in his forties. It bothered me from time to time…but mostly, I was wrapped up in my own life.

This whole new world was so different from anything I had ever known. I still couldn't believe that I was getting paid to play music every night and go to the beach every day. I could go to Cleveland whenever there was a good show at the theater because I had the money to do as I pleased. At sixteen, in this summer of '42, I was living a fantastic life.

The dance hall was totally different than those in the nightclubs we had played. It was a huge, covered, outdoor hall with a raised bandstand at one end of a round dance floor big enough for hundreds of people. This was "park plan" dancing — a dime a dance. A customer (mostly men but some women) would buy a string of tickets at ten cents each and then ask someone to dance. Each ticket was good for one dance set which consisted of two tunes. The dance floor was surrounded by a railing with several gates. You and your partner waited at the gate until the set was over and the dance floor had been cleared. Then the attendant at the gate took your ticket and let you in for the next set. There were four or five gates, with a constant stream of people coming and going through the gates all night long. It wasn't unlike an elegant roller rink.

It was awesome watching so many people dancing at the same time. The bandstand was set above the floor about four feet, so we looked down on the dancers. I loved the constant motion of them turning first one way then the other, skirts swishing back and forth with each turn to the rhythm of the music. Slow dances or up-tempo swing dances — we called it jitter-bugging, and soon everyone would — were equally interesting. I wanted so much to dance like that but the only partner I could find was Hilda. People thought nothing of girls dancing with each other in those days. But our only chances to dance were usually when the band was setting up in a club and there was jukebox music in the background. Then we could dance for fun. The dancing itself was the important thing, and we took every opportunity to do it.

There were no intermissions on this gig and in a short time this began to take its toll. We all got sore lips. Those of us in the reed section were probably the hardest hit because when you play a valve instrument the music you project is determined by the way you place your lips on the mouthpiece. I probably had it a little easier than most because with a saxophone your fingers can hit the right notes no matter what. But at one point I discovered blood on my reed and mouthpiece so I tucked a piece of Kleenex between my lip and teeth so that the reed rested on the wet Kleenex and gave me some relief. Once again Edna, Freddie, and Mack came to the rescue. They started playing one set by themselves so that the rest of us could take a five-minute break.

In time we found we could do this with each section. The sax section would play a set, then the brass would do the same. Sometimes Freddie would play a set with Edna and Mack, then a set with Edna and Mackie. Or Phyliss would take over the drums to give Mack a break. Freddie got a break once in awhile when Edna played the piano so Arthella (trumpet) and Hilda (sax) could sing a set. Sound confusing? It was, but it worked. All we knew was that the music had to keep going no matter what. We were checked every night by the owners to see what kind of crowds we were drawing — to make sure the dance floor was full every set. I wonder if older musicians could have played that gig? It was hard work, but we had our days on the beach to make up for it.

After about a month, Freddie started scheduling rehearsals every night after the job. We would end the last set, take a break to freshen up and change our clothes, then come back to the dance hall and rehearse until around three a.m. We did a lot of groaning about this, but it was really the only way. The dance hall would have been too hot during the day. And, of course, we didn't suffer too much since we spent our afternoons on the beach. Freddie was concerned that we were spending too much time in the hot sun during the day. He was afraid that all those hours on the beach were draining our strength.

Freddie decided we weren't getting enough rest and insisted that we go to bed right after rehearsals. To enforce the rule, he and Arthella would drive up and down the main street looking for us. If he hadn't been wearing sunglasses early in the morning — and drinking a little — and driving a big Buick Roadmaster, he might have spotted us now and then. But we always saw him first and ducked out of sight, so he never caught us breaking curfew.

I loved being on the beach, listening to the soothing sound of the waves lapping the sand. I would watch the huge freighters passing far out on the lake and wonder where they were going. One afternoon the weather turned really weird. The sky became ugly with green and gray clouds twisting and rolling toward us. The lifeguards ordered everyone out of the water and most retreated from the beach to take cover. But I was too fascinated to leave. I stood on the sand and watched two water spouts out near a pair of passing freighters. I had no idea of the danger involved. Then the wind started blowing so hard the sand stung my legs. I had to shield my eyes and run for shelter. I joined a group of people inside a beach restaurant and watched the storm through the windows until it blew over.

Although Freddie insisted that the sun sapped our strength, I always came to work feeling rested. I would stay at the beach until about four and then walk to The Farm House, stopping only for a slice of pizza or a chocolate eclair. I would try to get dibs on the bathroom before anyone else, have a nice bath, and then crash for an hour or so. We all came alive about dinner time, which was at six or seven. We went to Pera's Restaurant for our evening meal. What was nice for us (and the Peras) was that we could just sign our checks. My dinner almost every night of the week was a hot-beef sandwich with mashed potatoes and gravy. And by now I had learned to like coffee. For dessert I usually had a sundae made with chocolate ice cream topped with cherries. Geneva-on-the-Lake opened up a whole new menu for me. My mother had always made sure we ate good healthy food; we lived off the land when I was young. Even though we lived in town, we had a garden that produced fresh vegetables and our fruit came from cherry, apple, and plum trees on our property. But now, I was eating things I had never seen or smelled before. I was also gaining weight rather rapidly. I went through three bathing suits that summer. I was tan and preferred to think I had a healthy look. Eating was just part of the fun.

Thinking back, it might have been one of the reasons we were working here: If we were willing to live at The Farm House and eat every meal at the same restaurant, there was probably very little actual cash involved. In other words, Freddie had probably cut a deal to get us this resort job. But I, for one, wasn't complaining.

Hilda and I still had enough money to go into Cleveland once in a while to shop or go to the theater. If we heard of a big band playing a stage show, most of our band would go together to the city for a matinee. That's where I first saw Les Brown and His Band of Renown, and Frank Sinatra, who was then singing with Tommy Dorsey. Stage shows were wonderful. There were always special acts featured — singers, dancers, magicians, comedians, and, of course, the band and their own special entertainment. Les Brown had his brother "Stumpy" who was funny and entertaining. The stage shows, the shopping — it was all just grand.

We were learning to play the same music being made popular by the big-name bands and singers. Our own theme song, "Moonglow," had been popularized as the theme song of another band back in the thirties. "Star Dust" was perennially popular, as were "I'll Never Smile Again," "Moonlight Serenade," "This Love of Mine," and many other ballads. And there were many up-tempo numbers, including "String of Pearls," "Woodchopper's Ball," and "In the Mood." We found that we had to shorten a lot of the tunes for our gig at Geneva-on-the-Lake. The two songs per set were timed to get dancers quickly on and off the floor. That was the formula for park-plan dancing.

Hilda and I spent a lot of our money on clothes. Probably the craziest thing we bought were jackets copied after the famous zoot suits of that time. The guys who wore those suits — with their very long jackets and big pockets — usually had a long chain fastened to their belts that draped down and back up into their pants pockets. We didn't do the chain thing because we usually wore skirts. It was enough that we had these really cool jackets to wear to school when we went back to Frankfort.

That summer offered me another first. Every day we saw the same guys on the beach. Most of them were employed by the same people who employed us. They were lifeguards, waiters, bartenders. One guy in particular was very attentive to me. Tony — who was from Ashtabula and was at the resort every day — waited almost every night for me to get off work. We would hang out with some of the band or go walking on the beach. He was one passionate Italian and could not or would not understand that I liked him but not in a serious romantic way. I also had other responsibilities (I may have neglected to tell him). I had to go back and finish high school.

Hilda had a cute guy interested in her also. He was an extremely handsome lifeguard. Their relationship was going along very nicely until this guy's little brother decided he wanted to date Hilda. The older brother stepped aside and Hilda was crushed.

Our boyfriends were really sweet men but when the season ended and we packed up to go back to Indiana, the summer romances were soon forgotten. Hilda and I returned to Frankfort High School, and Freddie's band prepared for a USO tour. I was envious that Hilda would graduate in only one more year; I just couldn't wait two years. The band would surely forget about me by then.

I suddenly remembered that I had started first grade in January, which meant I was a mid-year student and just might have enough credits to graduate in '43 instead of '44 if I did a little extra work. The principal agreed to let me double up on two of my subjects so that I would have the credits I needed to graduate in '43. I was elated: Hilda and I could rejoin the band at the same time.

It was a great junior/senior year for me. I was still in the school dance band and got to participate in the big event of the year, the annual Big Broadcast. My picture was in the newspaper along with Julia, the girl who planned that year's program. It was wonderful being on stage again; I had learned to love it. Rosie, one of my classmates and a friend since first grade, was chosen to be the leader of the dance band. She was fantastic. She was so cute and bouncy — perfect for the part.

The year went by quickly. While all the other seniors were out having a good time, I had to work hard to make sure I finished enough credits to graduate. Finally I had only one credit to make up and of all things it was in music. For some reason I chose to learn to transpose music. Well, I wasn't getting it. Somehow I got through the class, though my music teacher was not thrilled with having to coach me until the last minute.

But I would have done anything to get that last credit. My only regret later was that I had changed classes at the same time that pictures were scheduled to be taken for our annual school book. I was unable to be officially recorded in either class. I wished I had planned it a little bet-ter. I would have liked having my picture taken with the class of '43.

TEXAS TOMMY
And His Wonder Horse Baby Doll

The Vogue Terrace
McKeesport, Pennsylvania

THE VOGUE TERRACE WAS A LARGE NIGHTCLUB IN A COUNTRY setting with a hotel on the second floor. It wasn't a great hotel, though it might have been at one time. Not that it mattered to us. The large rooms with their high ceilings and wooden floors and old-fashioned bathrooms were homey. The beds weren't exactly recent fixtures but the sagging mattresses and mismatched bedding were at least clean.

We liked it because with the nightclub and our rooms in the same building we could unpack our clothes and instruments and stay put. There was a big dining room and a kitchen with a full-time cook who appeared to be employed just for the band and the show people and some of the other help who lived there. Sometimes on nice days several of us would hike down the road to a little sandwich shop just for something different to do. After work we enjoyed being in the dining room with the show people for a late-night snack, or just to talk into the wee hours.

Occasionally we had big bonfires outside. Those were special times to be together, tell stories, and get to know each other better and just be close. It felt like a big family. Some of us had started on the road so young that we had missed the rituals of the autumn season. I especially missed spending Saturdays raking leaves and, in the evenings, having bonfires and tossing in a few apples to roast. My dad usually cut some long sticks for the marshmallows. Why did they taste so good, all burned to a crisp?

Some pretty elaborate shows were staged at the Vogue Terrace. It was located not far from Pittsburgh, but judging from the crowds we must have drawn people from all over the area. It was a beautiful setting at night. The room was terraced with rows of small tables, each with a white tablecloth and a small lamp for an intimate and cozy look. The round dance floor was surrounded on one side by the rows of tables, and on the other side by a bandstand raised off the floor about three feet. The evening's entertainment always followed a simple but firm formula. The band would play a set of four dance numbers followed by a fifteen-minute break, and then another set of four numbers. The idea was to encourage people to dance by starting out with a slow ballad or two, something sentimental. Sometimes someone would make a special request like "Star Dust." We must have played that a thousand times. After the slow tunes we would up the tempo and end with a barn burner. That would make everyone happy and also very thirsty, so that during the fifteen-minute break they would order drinks to get them through the next set. It was Freddie's job to read the crowd and determine what kind of music they liked. He was usually right.

In a nightclub setting like that there were also two floor shows every night, one at about ten p.m. and the other at midnight. After the second dance set, Freddie would announce the stars of the show to be performed following the break. That, of course, was what people came for — a full evening of entertainment. After the second floor show, the crowd usually began thinning out. Those who remained would be dancing slower, holding each other closer, and not wanting the music to end.

I liked watching the people. As an evening wore on, they revealed so much of themselves. I suppose the drinking contributed a little, but these were emotional times. You could tell the couples who had only a short time together before the man was to be shipped out. Or the couples who had just been reunited after being separated for a long time.

Some women came in groups dressed in very fashionable dresses or suits, high heels, and even hats and gloves. They danced with each other, probably to be seen, and it worked because they were always noticed by the men who came alone. Because of the war, there was a shortage of men so it wasn't at all unusual for women to dance together. It seemed the natural thing to do in those days.

From where I sat, I could see the joy, the excitement, the tears — all the emotions music could evoke in people. The music always had a message. Songs like, "Don't Sit Under the Apple Tree with Anyone Else but Me" and "Sentimental Journey" reflected the mood of many people — lyrics that made promises or asked you to wait or to remember. Many of those songs are being played again today, I notice.

When we were booked into a club that had floor shows, it was usually for at least one and sometimes two weeks. Getting ready for a new show required a lot of work; with only a couple days to get ready, it took hours and hours of rehearsing. There were even times when we had only a single afternoon to pull a show together for that night. Dancers had to learn cues and perfect tempos. Singers had it even harder because they had to learn not only tempos but key changes. Some songs were arranged in the most difficult keys we had ever encountered. If there was time, Freddie and Edna would stay up late into the night rewriting arrangements so we could read them more easily. Those two could sight read almost anything. When we performed we sometimes got hopelessly lost, with not a clue as to where we should be, and Freddie would hold his trumpet with one hand, playing it as loudly as he could, while trying to cue us in by flailing his free arm. Thank God Edna could interpret Freddie's motions and our drummer could make enough noise and play well enough to cover for us until a lead horn could find the right place to pull us back in.

Even when we made mistakes, we still looked good. Freddie's insistence that we dress in matching outfits paid off. It was not easy to find stores that offered thirteen gowns exactly alike, but we managed to locate some very pretty outfits. The make-up we wore seemed heavy but under the strong stage lights it looked natural. Edna had been a hairdresser in her earlier career, so she was often called on to do hairstyling for those of us who were not quite so adept at it. I loved doing my hair. Once away from home, I alternated between very blonde and dark brown, depending on my mood and the style I wanted.

As we worked more and needed more wardrobe, we were able to choose gowns for different settings. We had gray flannel suits for a relaxed daytime look. Nightclubs required a more formal look. The only mistake we made was buying long black floor-length dresses that left us looking colorless. In later years it was hard for me to accept the informal attire of young musicians in their mismatched shirts and blue jeans. It reflected an every-man-for-himself attitude, which most people seemed to take for granted, but which I thought was very unprofessional. My sons, who are both musicians, and I had many arguments about this. Even my husband would have to conform to this way of dressing when he played with younger musicians.

Some wonderful show people performed at the Vogue Terrace. "The Pin-Up Girls" were a roller-skating act. They brought their own circular skating pad to cover an area of the dance floor. Confined to that small circle, their performance seemed all the more intricate. Their skating was billed in a local entertainment magazine as "fast and extremely interesting, offering tricks on rollers that one would hardly expect women to do."

"The Kurtis Marionettes" were different than any act we had seen. Mr. Kurtis and Mr. Beans, as they were billed, were rather distinguished older men who used adult marionettes with slightly exaggerated figures for effect. Their May-West-type marionettes were clever and humorous, but never offensive. The act was a hit with the audience every night. After the show, when we all gathered in the dinning room for a sandwich, Mr. Kurtis and Mr. Beans would often read to us. I sometimes felt that they were treating us like the children they never had. They'd apparently spent their lives together with their marionettes. They wrote poems for us, too. I still have mine. It reads,

> To dear little Pat —
> who across from us sat
> From breakfast to dinner to midnight frat.
> The laughter we had — some good, some bad —
> Though I know we'll meet again,
> the parting is sad.

We didn't meet again after those shows at the Vogue, but I never forgot them.

Living so close together was trying at times. Out of necessity, we learned to accept whatever happened. The hardest times came when someone got sick. It didn't happen often but a case of the flu or a bad cold always left a hole in the band that had to be filled, usually by Freddie. One of the trombone players got sick while we were performing at the Vogue and was not able to play for a few days, so the rest of us had to work a little harder as a group. When the pressure got too great and we started feeling crowded, the Vogue Terrace was a wonderful place for getting out and hiking in the country to get away from everyone. I called it "getting aired out."

There were always new songs to learn and new people to work

with, and we never lacked for things to talk about. Just wandering in and out of each other's rooms kept things moving. Edna once told me that she enjoyed watching us younger girls laughing and having fun. Upstairs at the Vogue we were a little daring at times running around with our hair in rollers and wearing only our undies. Of course we thought we were hilarious.

Marlene, our lead alto sax player, always had a good feeling about every night. When things were too quiet, she would say, "I have this feeling that something exciting is going to happen tonight." And when an old friend or even one of our usual customers would appear, Marlene would say, "See, I told you so." If she forgot to bring it up, we would ask her if she had any good feelings about that night. She was a great lead alto player. She had the tone and the feeling for interpreting music consistently which made our sax section one of the best — and in a big band, section work is so important. I loved the way Marlene played and found it a joy to follow her lead. Quite often she would look at me after playing a pretty sax arrangement and say, "You knew just what I was thinking, didn't you?" That was Marlene all the way. And it was also the supreme compliment.

One of the most unusual acts we played for was Texas Tommy and His Wonder Horse, Baby Doll. I never did figure out the cues, but Texas Tommy had taught his horse to count, to know all the right yes-and-no answers to questions he would ask, and a few other humorous tricks. And as far as I know, Baby Doll never dumped on the stage. You gotta love a horse like that.

While at the Vogue Terrace we also worked with singers, dancers, and a magician whom I found very charming for the two weeks he was there. I don't remember exactly how I met him, but one day he caught me backstage snooping around in his bag of tricks. He let me know I had no business there, then asked me to go out. We drove far out in the country to find his favorite restaurant; we could have fried our own chicken quicker. He didn't want to be with the group after the show, saying he preferred to be alone with me, so that relationship was short-lived.

Once a gang of my friends from back home in Indiana came to visit us. It was a nice surprise but turned out to be a little awkward. I had dated one of the boys and he arrived prepared to ask some pretty serious questions. We were living such a different life than we had in Indiana. I don't think my old friends had any idea what my days and nights were now like. They seemed to be under the impression that those of us in the band were free to do whatever we wanted, but of course that wasn't so: This was our job, and we still had to be at rehearsals every afternoon and at work every night. My friends wanted to go out someplace after work but there just wasn't anyplace to go so we just drove around, much like we had back in Indiana. One night the guy I had dated back home asked me to marry him. I was shocked. There had never been any talk of this at home. I tried to be funny and make light of his proposal. I certainly wasn't ready for marriage. All I lived for was my career, which I felt fortunate to have. I didn't earn enough to support a husband, and my old boyfriend didn't seem capable of supporting us either.

After they left, I often wondered what my hometown friends told the folks back in Indiana. They weren't nearly as comfortable with musicians and show people as I was, and they probably thought I had too

much freedom for a girl my age. I hoped they at least recognized how hard the band was working in order to present the best show possible every night. It was important to me. I didn't want them to go home feeling shut out of my world, but I suppose they did feel that way.

•••

As nice as the Vogue Terrace was, it wasn't without problems — serious problems, we thought. At some point while playing the gig we realized that we were not being paid union scale. After a lot of secretive, late-night discussions, we decided we needed to do something about it. But we had to be careful: Some of the girls in the band would never dare complain — but wouldn't object if someone else did — and then there were the two girls who were involved romantically with Freddie. Those two, who we had already discovered were sometimes paid a little extra, could never know what we were up to.

On a free afternoon we went to the union hall in Pittsburgh and told the officials our suspicions. They asked for proof, such as pay slips to show over a period of time what we had been paid. They were very supportive and eager to help us, and promised that our names would never be revealed. They kept their word. After we brought them all the proof they needed, they filed a claim against both Freddie and the club, neither of which was paying union scale. After that the union upped the scale for the remainder of the time we were there. And Freddie had to pay back quite a large sum of money to the girls.

Of course the incident infuriated him. On nights when he was drinking on the job he would suddenly turn to one of us and shout, "Did *you* do it?" We all kept straight faces and said, "no." I don't think he ever found out, which surprised me. Even those girls who did not join our little band of rebels refused to tell on us. Phyliss and Mack never told, nor did Edna, though she worked more closely with Freddie than any of us.

There came a time when Edna's husband, J.D., arrived home from the service. I think Freddie was afraid Edna would leave the band so he hired J.D. as band manager. Edna was happy, J.D. was happy, and the rest of us were happy to have someone to help us while we traveled. And maybe Freddie was happy to have a man to talk to.

J.D. was an extremely handsome guy, which worried Edna a little. One day she came to our room and confided her suspicions: She had found a cigarette in the ashtray of their car that was not hers, and it had lipstick on it that was not hers. What should she do? We would do anything for Edna so we tried to come up with ideas that might be helpful. The best came from Beverly, our trombone player. She said the only thing to do was keep J.D. so tired that he wouldn't have the energy to even look at another woman. From then on when we went to work every night, there would be those knowing glances at Edna. If she was smiling, we knew the plan was working.

Always - Remember:

Life is a blend of
A bit of glad a
A pinch of c
A dash of s
A little

42

Evansville, Indiana

CAROLYN JANE WENT TO THE IVY LEAGUE AND PATSY WENT
on the road...

While I was on the road, the nightclub in Evansville seemed like
home territory because my cousin, Carolyn Jane, lived there and we were
able to spend time together shopping and being at her house for dinner
with my aunt and uncle. My aunt was a beautiful woman but the family
had not been very kind to her because she hadn't had much of an education. That didn't stop her from pursuing her ambitions, however. She had
gone to work selling Avon and was eventually made district manager. She
was so proud of her office when she showed it to me. She took a nice bottle of perfume out of the display case and gave it to me.

I was very comfortable visiting my aunt and uncle, but I later
wondered what they really thought of their niece playing in a nightclub
in the area outside of town called No Man's Land. It was in a disputed

area between Indiana and Kentucky where the liquor laws were a little vague. There was also gambling in the club, though I didn't know it at the time. I was so young and inexperienced that I just assumed everyone in the family was delighted that I had such a wonderful job. However, my aunt and uncle never came out to see the show or hear me play in the band.

My visits probably hastened Carolyn Jane's enrollment in an Ivy League college. She has always loved to sing and dance as much as I did: As children, when we spent summers on the farm, we were always putting on shows in the barn for Grandma. My aunt and uncle probably worried that under my bad influence their daughter would run off and join a band.

The club date in Evansville was our most difficult ever. We were hired to play for a dance troupe, and their music was almost impossible. "The Fire Dance" and "Maleguena" had to be rewritten so that we could read them. I could never understand why dancers required changes in key and tempo. Key changes can make the music more brilliant and thus more effective (that arrangement of "The Fire Dance" is memorable even today), but it sure makes the band's job tougher. The costumes worn by the dancers consisted of sheer bodysuits festooned with yards of flame-colored chiffon. As the dancers moved, the chiffon flowed in every direction, creating the illusion of flames dancing in wonderfully choreographed rhythms. It was beautiful but the music was so difficult it was hard for me to enjoy the dancers.

We rehearsed and rehearsed and in the end Freddie demanded that we all just watch him for cues and clues. Even with his cues and the simpler arrangement written by Freddie and Edna, the brass and sax sections often fell apart. Freddie continued to play holding his trumpet with one hand and directing us with the other and nodding his head in the direction of the section that was supposed to come in while moving that trumpet up and down to keep time rhythms. Somehow he got us through it all and the dancers never complained. It was the truly professional people who never complained; the second-rate acts would always blame the band. No matter. Most people just wanted to dance and be happy and forget about the war for a few hours, and they were more than willing to overlook mistakes.

By now Hilda and I had learned how to smoke. We just couldn't do without those cigarettes. And why not? Everyone was doing it then. The American people sent them by the tons overseas to our servicemen as a gesture of love and thoughtfulness. Good cigarettes were in short supply here at home but some enterprising person had come up with these neat, inexpensive machines so we could roll our own. So, of course, I bought one and a can of tobacco and papers and became very adept at making my own cigarettes.

You've heard that old joke about Prince Albert tobacco? As kids we used to call the local grocer on the phone and ask him if he had Prince Albert in the can. When he answered yes, we would shout, "Well, let him out!" And of course we would hang up and laugh ourselves silly. Well, that was my brand when I could get it.

While rehearsing at the club one day I asked a waiter to please bring me some weeds. That was the common slang word for cigarettes then. He was gone for a very long time and when he returned he was half hidden in the shadows of the stage and motioned for us to come backstage with him. His arms were full of what looked like stalks of weeds. I had no idea what he was doing, but one of the older girls did. She ordered him to get that stuff away from us. I still didn't understand what "stuff" it was until someone practically drew me a picture. It was marijuana, of course. We were lucky we didn't get busted.

The master of ceremonies and comedian of the show became a good friend. We enjoyed each other's company, but never in the romantic sense. After work at night we would take long walks down by the river. There had been some major flooding and people were monitoring the river day and night to see if the water had receded. One or two nights we were unable to make it to No Man's Land because of high water. We talked forever on those nights. Jimmy was married and he told me of his life and advised me on ways I could make a good life for myself when I got married. Some of the girls in the band did not approve of the time Jimmy and I spent together, but our friendship was truly innocent. I've learned that there are times when having a good friend is better than having a lover. On the last night of the show when he said his good-byes to everyone, he blew me a kiss and gave me a picture of himself. He had written a lovely poem on the back of it.

Theaters in the larger cities often offered afternoon matinees that included a big band with its specialty numbers and an assortment of acts, usually dancers, a singer, and maybe a comedian. Les Brown and his comic brother Stumpy were playing in Evansville when we were there and we went to the show every afternoon that we could. We had seen the show in Cleveland, Akron, and other cities — enough times to be noticed by the boys in the Band of Renown. When we lined up in the front-row seats we got stares from them, and they would nod to one another as if to say, "check it out, man." They probably thought we were groupies following them all over the Midwest, which we found amusing. We never had the chance to meet them. It was more fun that way. We would show up again the next day, and they never did figure out who we were.

We often met other musicians and show people in the lobby of our hotel as they were going to work or out to eat. They were always fascinated by the idea of a bunch of girl musicians on the road. If they took the time to catch our show, it was the same thing over again — "You really are good for a bunch of women." The only musicians I didn't have a hard time with were singers. Singers were an important part of the entertainment in every band. The girl singers, dressed in lovely formals, sat at one side of the stage always smiling and always ready to sing. Every band had a girl singer. And most of them had male singers also. When he became the rage, Frank Sinatra changed the whole image of singers and bands. Before, the band was always the star and the singer played a supporting role. But now Sinatra was the star. All he had to do was sing "There Are Such Things" and it would send shivers up your spine and make all the young girls scream. Being blessed with good looks and a great voice made all the difference. Always has.

The Persian Terrace
Syracuse, New York

IN THE WINTER OF 1942–43, WE WERE BOOKED INTO WHAT WAS supposed to be a simple job. It turned out the posh hotel in Syracuse was more elegant than any place we had ever been.

The Persian Terrace was a dining room and ballroom that looked like something out of a movie set. It had sheer curtains and draperies covering most of the walls and beautiful damask tablecloths on every table with candlelight and crystal chandeliers. We had special new gowns for this job and Freddie had turned us all into ladies. No more bobby socks and hair in pin curls, we were supposed to walk into the hotel wearing our Sunday best. The gowns were perfect for this setting: long flowing skirts made of pale green chiffon, with tops of a light coral color, a sweetheart neckline embroidered with the pale green of the skirts. We each wore either gold or silver slippers. Even Mack would make her appearance wearing silver slippers (though once behind the drums her loafers were an absolute necessity). The gowns were the prettiest we had ever owned, and with thirteen women all dressed alike, it made quite an elegant picture.

Several afternoons a week and on weekends, we were required to play a tea dance: a polite society dance with no loud music or fast tempos. Every evening except Sundays we played a dinner dance.

While our audience seemed to like our performance, no one ever spoke to us. If there was a request for a song, a waiter delivered it to Freddie. (This is where I learned what being part of the help was all about.) But the job was easy and we were paid well. Just watching the beautiful people every night, how they dined and how they danced, was awesome. I wondered if this was the way they lived all the time, and thought how different it was from how I was brought up in my railroad town in Indiana. I marveled at the way the waiters bowed with every order they took from their customers.

We didn't get to sample such luxury. We stayed in a modest hotel downtown and ate at the coffee shop there. I presumed bacon wasn't rationed at the Persian Terrace like it was at our little coffee shop.

We spent our free time shopping and enjoying the city. I had seen someone wearing a pair of shoes I really liked, and decided I wanted a pair like them. So that became my quest in Syracuse. I shopped until I found exactly what I wanted. As usual, Hilda was there for me when it came to shopping. The only time she backed off was when she wanted to put a fur coat in layaway and was told she'd have to send weekly payments until it was paid off.

One day Mackie, our bass player, met a young man who seemed nice. We all enjoyed his good nature and thought that he and Mackie made an ideal couple. But he disappeared suddenly, without any message to Mackie. These kinds of things happened on the road.

About that time I met a very charming man, a captain in the M.P. division — military police. He asked me to go out to dinner with him and

I did. I felt so safe with this man. He was tall, and in his uniform, exuded authority. He always took me to very nice places for dinner. I'm sure he liked me but he sometimes seemed annoyed that I ordered milk with my dinner instead of a drink.

Over dinner we would talk about life on the road and the girls in the band and the men they were dating. But something about our conversations bothered me. He asked so many questions that finally I became uncomfortable and told him that it was none of his business. Then he started playing hardball. He told me that I better answer him or else. I insisted he tell me why he wanted to know so much about the girls and their boyfriends. Finally he admitted that he was trying to find Mackie's boyfriend. It turned out he was AWOL, not for the first time, and that he was very good at dodging the MPs. Now I was angry because I felt used. I told him tersely what I knew, which wasn't much: The guy liked Mackie, he was nice, he split. That was it.

I didn't see the captain for a few days, and when he finally reappeared he told me that he had caught his man. He surprised me by asking me out a few more times. We maintained a friendship but eventually he started suggesting a more permanent commitment, which was not what I wanted. We didn't stay in touch for long after that.

After the band closed in Syracuse, we packed up and headed for our next job, in Akron, Ohio, to play at a nightclub called the Continental Grove. During the drive we got caught in a fierce blizzard and had to stop in a village not far outside of Syracuse. We actually had to abandon our cars on the road and check into a small hotel, the only one in town. It was like a scene out of a movie — and not the same movie featuring The Persian Terrace. The lobby was packed with people who were also stranded, all huddled around in chairs, crowded onto an old couch and on the floor in front of the fireplace. Every inch of space was occupied. Thanks to Freddie's persuasiveness, we got a couple of rooms. We slept crammed together on cots and beds.

The roads were closed for miles around. For days no cars could move and the entire region was brought to a halt. Our money ran out and we had no way of getting more. The snow finally stopped but snow removal was slow and our cars were still buried in drifts. Freddie somehow found a guy with heavy equipment who agreed to take him to our cars, unload the instruments, and bring them to the hotel. After that we sang for our supper. We set up a bandstand in the dining room. Then we dressed in our formals, the pretty ones we had worn in Syracuse, put on our stage makeup, and played for the people in the hotel. Talk about an appreciative audience. The guests had grown bored to death and were desperate for entertainment, and Freddie was relieved to be able to defray some of our hotel bill.

Even before these spontaneous shows, we girls had developed cabin fever. One day, for lack of anything better to do, we hiked through the snow to a nearby hill and just stood there screaming and laughing until we had blown off steam and worked off some tension. Our only other entertainment was visiting the hardware store and hanging out talking with the owner. We certainly were happy to be working again.

When the roads were finally cleared we headed for Akron where we were scheduled to open right after Christmas. But we weren't out of trouble yet. We hit icy roads where we had to slow down to keep from sliding into the ditches, and our old Buick Roadmasters just couldn't make it over the mountains. We waited for help to come along, but nobody else was foolish enough to be traveling. Finally Freddie said, "Okay, all the heavies get out and start pushing." That meant those of us who were not quite as "frail" as others. Hilda and I were among the first out. In those days we had galoshes rather than the neat boots I own today. They were unattractive but very efficient and had great traction. It was a good thing, because we needed all the advantage we could get against those heavy cars. We put our shoulders to the bumpers and pushed, first one Buick, then the other, over hill after hill. Maybe it was our sniping at each other that gave us the strength, or maybe it was Freddie's sarcastic comment about "heavies," but somehow we made it. By the time we got to Akron we were exhausted, fighting among ourselves, mad at Freddie, and it was nearly Christmas.

Even living together like we did, we still got lonely and homesick during the holidays. Once, I thought if I could only go to church then everything would be better. But it wasn't. I found a church at random, but when I sat in the pew all I could think about were my family and how my little brother used to make everyone laugh in church by just looking at them with his big brown eyes. The memory of it caused me to cry. During holidays I made a lot of long distance calls to my parents and that seemed to get me through the lonely days.

Freddie recognized our problem and on Christmas Eve in Akron he and Arthella, the woman he was closest to, threw a big party for us. I don't know how they found the time to shop and plan the party, but they surprised us with presents for everyone and loads of food. It turned out to be a pretty decent Christmas after all.

I have often wondered how Freddie did it, riding herd on thirteen women, most of us teenagers. He could hardly ever get away from us, even to spend time with the woman who seemed to be his secret love. We were very hard on him for that. The rest of us met people we cared about and others that were just fun to be around, but not Freddie — we wouldn't let him. So he was usually alone — except when we were on stage and the curtain went up and we were one again.

The Continental Grove
Akron, Ohio

AFTER OUR HARROWING TRIP FROM SYRACUSE AND THEN THE Christmas party Freddie threw for us, we began rehearsing for a big New Year's celebration at the Continental Grove in Akron. Freddie had always told Edna exactly what he wanted and how the band should sound and she would write it for us. But now we were branching out into stock arrangements — written to sound just like the band that had made a particular song popular. "String of Pearls," for instance, was written to sound like Glenn Miller's arrangement, right down to the two sax solos and the clarinet lead his band was known for. When people asked us to play "String of Pearls," they expected us to play it the way Glenn Miller did. And when we succeeded and the audience applauded our efforts, it was truly a kick.

The first rehearsal for the new floor show went beautifully. We were all waiting on stage when a tall, handsome Chinese man walked in.

He smiled and greeted us with, "Hi, girls. I'm Jack Soo." I had no idea the treat we were in for. He handed Freddie his music, and, in turn, Freddie passed out our parts. These were special arrangements written for vocals and they actually turned out to be easier to read than our usual arrangements. The rehearsal was fun and interesting and left us in awe of this man who had such an incredible singing voice.

We worked with Jack Soo and also a trio of dancers on special numbers for the New Year's Eve bash. Our music included show tunes written to show off either the sax section or the brass and our singers. Our drummer, Mack, could put on a show that many people said was equal to Gene Krupa's. She had that kind of energy.

It turned out Jack Soo was not only a very special performer, but he was also carrying around a secret that must have been hard for him. I found out much later that he was actually Japanese American. In those days Japanese people were not popular. After Jack's death in 1979, I donated a signed photo of him to a Smithsonian exhibit honoring him for his contributions to the entertainment world. The curator of the Community Life division of the Smithsonian told me that Jack Soo's real surname had been Suzuki.

After the war, Jack's singing career took off. Then he turned to acting, and much later became popular on television's *Barney Miller* show. You might remember him.

After the successful New Year's show, our band became regulars at the Continental Grove. We would be booked there for a couple weeks at a time, then hit the road for another club someplace or for a string of one-nighters. But I always looked forward to returning to Akron. I liked seeing familiar faces on the dance floor and the smiles from people waving to let us know they had come back to see us. And each new show was interesting. One featured Emmett Kelly, the famous clown. I was excited about playing for someone so well known, but he turned out to be an ornery old coot more interested in the girls than we were in him. There was something about a guy made up like a clown that just didn't appeal to me. But he was funny on stage and the audience loved him.

There was one face in the crowd that I started looking for every night. The first time I saw him I thought he was about the greatest looking guy ever. He was tall, with dark wavy hair, big brown eyes, and very sensual lips that looked always ready to smile. I really wanted to meet him.

Finally, at one of our intermissions, he moved in and started a conversation with one of the other girls. Damn! I was jealous, and I hadn't even met him yet. Next intermission, same thing. He talked to everyone in the band except me and they all thought he was really neat. His name was Donald, they said. Swell. So what was wrong with me? And why was I acting like this? It wasn't like me.

After the gig, while we were packing up, he was suddenly standing before me. He asked if I would like to go out for a bite to eat. Trying to be cool, I said rather hesitantly, "That might be nice." He said he would wait for me in the bar. I left the club through the downstairs bar and he wasn't there. I was crushed. I went back to the hotel with the girls and changed into slacks and a sweater. Freddie always wanted us to change into our street clothes before going out.

I was ready to leave with the girls when there was a knock at the door. It was Donald. He wanted to know why I hadn't waited for him. What had happened was, I had left by the downstairs bar but he had waited in the upstairs bar. I was glad he hadn't given up on me.

We left for our date. I thought we would join the usual group, but Donald led me to his car. That made me a little nervous. Where was my back-up team? I got in and he drove to a drive-in restaurant. Remember the cute waitresses in short skirts and bobby socks who took your order and then picked it up after you had eaten and honked the horn? I ordered a hamburger with onions. Donald sort of raised his eyebrows. That was like saying, "Not tonight, honey." So he ordered onions, too. After we had eaten, we made small talk while he drove around, ending up finally in a rather secluded place. Regardless of the onions, I found that I liked being close to him. He felt good and he smelled good and I was happy with that. He looked at me for awhile and finally said, "I just don't get it." What he didn't get was that I wasn't ready for anything other than just dating. I asked him to drive me back to my hotel. I thought I probably would never see him again.

But I would. One night on stage, our saxophone section had gone out front to perform. We were doing a beautiful and intricate number when the sax strap that fit around my neck to hold my horn in place broke and my horn went crashing to the floor. I was totally embarrassed but I picked up my horn and held it so that it looked like I was playing, though I wasn't. Donald was there and saw the whole thing. I was sure he would never want to be around a klutz like me.

But Donald did come back. He seemed happy to be with clumsy me on my own turf with all the girls around. We had a lot of fun together. He was funny and loved to sing and clown around with everyone.

He had a cottage on a lake near Akron where we all went when we were in Akron during warm weather. We spent more and more time together. He came to visit me once when we played the Vogue Terrace in McKeesport at Christmas time. The band lived upstairs at the club but there were no extra rooms for guests so Donald and I could find no place to be alone. On Christmas Day we sat in his cold car and exchanged gifts but it was just too cold to be close and loving. On a rare vacation he came to Indiana to meet my parents. He and my brother were just terrible at dinner, saying and doing outrageous things that made everyone laugh — but embarrassed me. They shared the same room that night and seemed to have a great time together.

In Akron, Donald took me to visit his own family. He gave me more attention and love than I had ever known and I was sure I was madly in love with him. But I still had this other love — the band and the excitement of traveling and working with other entertainers. Donald and

I did agree to a sort of engagement: He tore a dollar bill in two and gave me half. If either of us ever decided it was over, we were to send our half back and there would be no questions asked.

Donald was not all that happy in Akron so he decided to go to California to make his fortune and then send for me. He didn't write and I was devastated for awhile. Some time later I found out from his brother that his life out there had not been easy and he didn't want me to know. Donald's family wished I would wait for him just a little while longer, but by then I had put my half of the dollar bill away and was engaged to be married to a saxophone player with Bob Chester's band.

Norfolk, Virginia

I REMEMBER NORFOLK AS A COASTAL CITY SPREAD DOWN A single street that was so long it seemed to have no beginning and no end. Everywhere you looked were sailors — lots of them. Most of them were American, but there were many French sailors as well. Those cowboys had an "attitude," as we would call it now. They stared openly at Hilda and me and whistled and made remarks and pointed. Considering their reputation, we didn't want to even look in their direction.

But the American sailors — well, no secrets there. They were funny. You had to love them; at a distance, of course.

We were booked into a nightclub in Norfolk. Besides playing the club every night, we also played some daytime shows at the Navy base. It was always a thrill to play for people who cheered you on and made you feel like your performance was the most wonderful show in the world, and it was interesting seeing the sailors on their own turf. But something was missing. What was it? *The ties.* While they were on base, they did not wear their black ties. They couldn't get off the base without them. No tie, no pass. It was a simple but effective way of controlling who left the base.

I was surprised one night when Hollace, a friend from home, came to the club to see me. I was happy to see a familiar face and impressed by how good he looked in his navy uniform. We had dated at home but it had never been really serious. My favorite story about Hollace was of the night my mother came out on the porch and told me it was getting late and suggested it was time for him to go home. He chose to ignore my mother. After a while she came out again, this time on the pretense of watering the lawn. When it looked like Hollace still wasn't planning on leaving, Mother just sort of flipped the nozzle of the hose at him. He in turn grabbed the hose and sprayed her with it. No one had ever done such a thing to my mother. But for some reason she thought it was funny and they had an all-out water fight. In the end, Hollace let her win and that was that. We laughed about it for weeks.

After Hollace discovered I was playing in Norfolk, he came to see me whenever he could get off the base. We enjoyed walking around the city and being together. One night out of the blue, he asked me to marry him. I didn't think he was serious and sort of brushed the question aside. The next night as we were walking along hand in hand, his girl-friend from home and her mother showed up right on the sidewalk in front of us. Needless to say, it was an awkward situation. Hollace walked me to my rooming house and said goodbye and later I learned that he had married the girlfriend. It didn't matter to me, of course. I was still mar-ried to my job.

At the club one night I ordered a Coke and became upset when the bartender shortchanged me. The bar was very busy and I wasn't com-fortable complaining but I knew I was right. I didn't let the bartender off the hook until he had handed over the rest of my money. He apologized and said that it was an honest mistake, then asked if he could walk me home after the gig. The girls and I lived in run-down rooming houses close to the club, not the best housing in Norfolk. The beds were clean but the little critters that had taken up residence were more than a nuisance. Hilda became so upset one night about the six-legged guests in our room that she fled to one of the other rooms and slept with the girls there.

Anyway — the rooming house was across the street from a schoolhouse. After the club closed, my friend the bartender and I would sit close to each other on the school steps in the shadows and talk. He always carried a small zippered bag but I didn't think much about it. One night we heard a rustling noise in the dark near us. In an instant he opened the bag and pulled out a knife. "Let's go," he ordered. He grabbed me by the arm and pulled me quickly away from the steps and onto the sidewalk under a streetlight and then walked me across the street to my rooming house. I thought he was overreacting until I learned that his zippered bag was packed with money from the bar, which he took home at night and deposited in the bank in the morning. He wasn't as appealing after I had learned that.

Other things did appeal to Hilda and me. Norfolk's downtown had many wonderful shops. We were shameless the way we tried on clothes for hours, never thinking that the poor sales ladies had other things to do than try to sell clothes to teenaged girls who were obsessed with shopping. I bought a brown dress that I didn't even like because I felt guilty about taking so much of the clerk's time. I later bought shoes to match. I had never owned more than two pairs of shoes until I went on the road. Freddie was strict about limiting us to one suitcase each, and eventually I had to ship many of my lovely clothes home, where most of them disappeared into the sibling vortex.

We met many interesting people with wonderful stories to tell. One night at an intermission, this handsome black lieutenant started chatting with some of us and told us that he had just become engaged to be married. The part I loved was the way he described his fiance as being so beautiful — the color of coffee with just a little cream. It was very romantic to see a man so deeply in love.

During this stage of the war, many civilians who owned their own boats volunteered to cruise along the coast and report anything suspicious. One man told us that it was common to see the periscopes of German submarines near the three-mile limit. He offered to take us all for a boat ride during the day to show us his territory. We accepted and it was exciting to look for submarines and listen to his stories about the spying going on right there off the coast of Virginia. We were so young that we didn't quite understood what it was all about. Even when we entertained wounded soldiers at army hospitals, we knew only that they were happy to see us and that our job was to entertain them and make that day something to write home about. We didn't really understand the realities of war, however. I doubt that we could have handled them.

Some men coped with their problems better than others. One such man was an officer who had lost an arm and wore a prosthesis. He told us that while he was standing in the aisle of a public bus, holding onto the overhead strap with his good arm, a woman turned to him and accused him of touching her derriere with his hand. He very graciously apologized and said, "Madame, I will be very happy to take the damned thing off if you like."

Our nightclub dates, in Norfolk and elsewhere, often included shows during the day for servicemen at nearby bases. Once we had to put a show together at the last minute, on the way to the base. We wore our gowns and carried our instruments onto the military bus, then rehearsed as we drove through town. We had no choice since army hospitals and navy bases didn't have dressing rooms or rehearsal halls set up for girl musicians. It was part of the job, after all, and we were willing to do just about anything to put on a good show.

Texas

Edna at the Plantation Club, Houston, 1943

THE BAND WENT ON A USO TOUR OUT WEST IN 1943. I WAS IN my senior year in high school and counting the days until I could graduate and join them. Their itinerary for January, February, and March was almost unbelievably full; they had maybe two or three days off during the month of January. I counted over eighty military bases on their tour. Had I known all the fun they would have, I would have quit school and joined them. Hilda tried but her parents wouldn't hear of it. Young girls in Frankfort, Indiana, didn't quit school in those days.

After I was finally able to rejoin the band in June, I got to see a little of the Southwest. One memorable gig was the Fat Stock Show in Dallas. That was *big*. Because we were there to entertain and also play for other entertainers, we really didn't have time to take it all in. The "palace" we played in was like an enormous barn with a large stage. We had a bit of a problem with the sound but I doubt that anyone else noticed. The place was not fancy. There were long tables with white paper covers set up around a big dance floor. People would eat and drink and dance and it seemed like everyone was talking all at once. There were other entertainers besides us but the only act I remember was a dancer whose routine was supposed to represent a horse. She mostly pranced around the stage with her hair flowing like a horse's mane and with a tail fastened to the rear of her costume. That seemed to be taking artistic license to the limit.

We played at another memorable dance hall in Houston. It was packed every night and on Sunday afternoons with dancers doing some of the most incredible swing dancing or jitter-bugging I had ever seen. The hall was hot but still those Texans would dance until they were ready to drop. It was a show every night watching the dancers swing and twirl and throw their partners over their shoulders and between their legs. It was wonderful how the excitement would build between the dancers and the band. They wanted the music hot, we gave them what they wanted, and they loved every minute of it.

It was hard enough getting used to Houston's heat and humidity, but what really upset me about Texas was when Phyliss found a scorpion under her bed. From then on I checked my clothes and shoes every time I got dressed and I don't think any of us slept soundly for the rest of our stay there. We Northern belles didn't adapt very well to those Texas critters.

Recently Hilda refreshed my memory about a gig we played in Fort Worth, at the very posh Colonial Country Club. I vaguely remember the rooms the band lived in. They were called sample rooms — big spaces that could be converted into show rooms for conventions or other events. In our case the club's management provided several beds and cots for each room. I think six of us shared a room: It was nice enough, clean and with lots of windows. That was important since Hilda and I were still learning how to smoke. We would wait until everyone was settled down at night and then we'd perch in a window and light up our cigarettes and blow the smoke outside. Hilda got really sick but she wouldn't give up. As we smoked we checked each other out to make sure we were doing it right. We wanted so much to look sophisticated. This was also when I decided I wanted to be a blonde. I bought a bottle of Marchand's Hair Color at the drugstore and lucky for me it changed my drab brown hair to a lovely golden blonde. At least I thought it was lovely. Freddie never commented on it.

One of my biggest thrills in Forth Worth was riding down on the elevator one day with the movie star Robert Taylor and his wife. About that same time, Hilda saw Tyrone Power. We decided there must be a theater nearby. It was thrilling to see movie stars so close. I was so awestruck that I couldn't even ask for an autograph. If I had tried, I probably would have said something really stupid anyway.

Then there was another small military base in Pecos, Texas. We were put up in barracks there, along with some of the WAC's — the Women's Army Auxiliary Corps. When we went to our assigned quarters, our bedding had been stacked on our cots. That was fine. We dutifully made up our beds. I was aware that some of the WAC's were snickering at us because we didn't know how to square those corners army style. One of our girls who was a master gave the rest of us a quick lesson so we would make a better showing the next time any of the WAC's were around to check us out. I still make my bed that way.

We didn't have a bathroom in our barracks and one night I really needed one badly. I went out searching, which I guess was something you didn't do there. Out of the pitch dark I heard this voice call, "Who goes there?" I very meekly replied that I was one of the girls in the band and that I needed to go to the bathroom. The guard let me pass. It was so dark out that I couldn't tell if I used the men's or women's, or even if there was a difference.

Texas was stranger than any place I had ever visited. Never

before had I seen so many miles and miles of flat land; it seemed to take forever to get from one place to another. And not being from Texas, we just didn't fit in. We were made to feel like outsiders, and I couldn't tell if it was because we were the help or because we were Northerners.

We played "Deep in the Heart of Texas" more than any other number.

The Blue Moon Nightclub
Wichita, Kansas

KANSAS WAS A DRY STATE. NOT THAT IT MATTERED — THE clubs seemed to flourish even without serving liquor. I found out how. They had very nice tables with clever little cubby holes built underneath. With a white tablecloth covering it, who knew? Customers paid a cover charge to get in and then ordered "set ups," which were lots of ice and any kind of soft drinks they wanted to mix with the bottles of liquor and wine they had smuggled in under their coats or in their purses. I don't know why anyone bothered to hide their bottles under the table, since everyone in the club was doing it. For that matter, I don't know why they bothered calling Kansas a dry state. You could buy anything to drink you wanted there.

The Blue Moon Nightclub had an unusually large dance floor. People there really loved to dance the whole night long. A lot of the same people came night after night and it was fun getting to know them. I got so I looked for certain people, partly just to see how they dressed. I noticed if the same outfit was worn more than once, and I noticed the trend in shoes — less and less leather was being used. Plastic was not yet in style but fabrics were being used in interesting ways. I had a pair of wonderful brown shoes that were made of a very durable gabardine-type material with brass nail heads around the platform sole and heel. That was a very hot style at the time.

At about ten o'clock every night we did a live broadcast from the Blue Moon. This was exciting. The music had to be timed just right for the half hour we were on the air. Freddie took his cues from the announcer in order to know when to have us fade in or out while the announcer was doing a commercial. We always started with our theme song, "Moonglow," playing it softly while we were being introduced, then going into our first number after we had been cued. Our announcer was a very handsome man who looked like the movie star I'd seen in Texas, Robert Taylor. Along with his good looks he had a talent for charming the audience into coming right up next to the bandstand so they were cheering and applauding at just the right moments. What a kick!

We had lovely new gowns for this gig so the whole presentation was perfect. The black taffeta skirts covered with black net and white tops with just a touch of red were formal but not at all stiff-looking, and flattered everyone in the band. We loved being invited back to play return engagements but we could only return to the Blue Moon when we happened to be in that part of the country. We played there maybe three times in all.

Though the term was covered in our contracts, we didn't really count on being affected by "acts of God." We were booked for some one-nighters and had just played a military base in Hutchinson, Kansas. After the gig we packed up and headed for Wichita, not knowing that the Arkansas River had flooded. The city of Wichita was high and dry, but the Blue Moon Nightclub was surrounded by water. Our contract's language basically put us on a paid vacation until the water receded enough to allow us to get to the club. There was very little for most of the girls to do since we didn't have boyfriends or much of a regular social life. (That is, except for one of our trombone players, Franny, who managed to have a tryst in a storage closet with a guy she met in the hotel.) Hilda and I opted for what we did best — shopping. Wichita had some wonderful shops, and I found a lovely navy blue wool dress that was trimmed in pearl buttons. Then I needed accessories to go with it, of course, so I bought red lizard shoes and a purse to match. The outfit was definitely a luxury, but I thought it was smashing. I came to feel the outfit was truly meant to be, because later it was what I chose to be married in. I wasn't aware of any rules then — like not wearing red shoes for your wedding. What was the old saying? Married in red, wish yourself dead? It never happened, I never did. And I loved those shoes.

So did my sister Phyllis. When she saw them, she took my red shoes to Lafayette, Indiana, where she was in nurse's training. Eventually I had to go there and raid her locker to liberate my shoes and other clothing she had "borrowed." I finally realized that my sister was envious of my seemingly glamorous life. Neither of us had ever owned many store-bought clothes, and Phyllis was keen to grab my "hand-me-downs." I don't think she really considered them secondhand clothing, though that was her argument when confronted for taking them.

Back in Wichita, the floodwaters finally receded, and the band returned to the Blue Moon for what would be our last gig there.

Washington, D.C.

I'LL NEVER FORGET NIGHTS IN OUR NATION'S CAPITOL IN THE '40s. Washington, D.C. was under a "brown-out" for most of the war. I had never seen anything like it. All the city lights were kept dim, like lamps that had been turned down for the night. No floodlights lit the Capitol or any other government building. The reason was simple — if enemy planes attacked they would have a harder time finding Washington in a brown-out. Everyone was a little afraid of air attacks, but in those days we still felt safe walking around in the city at night.

Freddie had booked us into the Uline Arena, a huge place used for all kinds of entertainment, including boxing matches, conventions, concerts, and political rallies. Our band was there for one reason: to keep people dancing.

While in Washington we lived in private homes in a lower-middle-class neighborhood close to the arena. Entertainers were often housed there. Hilda and I shared a room in a small house owned by a nice couple who were expecting a baby at any time. Hilda was always reminding me to be quiet and to keep our room neat so we wouldn't disturb our landlady. I remember the weather was very hot and our room upstairs never cooled down. Though our hosts never complained, the hours we kept must have been a little difficult for them. We were used to going out after work to have a bite to eat; we never got to bed early, and I'm sure we disturbed their sleep when we came home in the wee hours of the morning.

Uline Arena was packed every night. A lot of military men came to the dances, and of course we got to know some of them. Frannie, our trombone player, met two soldiers who were identical twins — even down to their military rank — and there was absolutely no telling them apart. One of them wanted to date Frannie, and the other wanted to go out with me. We went out quite a few times and were constantly entertained by the twins, who enjoyed the fact that we could not tell them apart. They were a lot of fun. Another girl met a young man who worked for a foreign diplomat. When Mr. Diplomat turned in for the night, the young man was allowed to drive his car, which happened to be a very long black limo. After our performances, we would all pile into the limo and drive wherever we wanted. The streets were practically empty because gas was rationed. Military police stopped us a few times but always let us go when they noticed the diplomatic plates on our car. They would say, "Have a good time, soldiers." And we did. We went sightseeing all over the city those nights. A favorite place was the Washington Monument, where we could wade in the cool water of the pool or just sit around laughing and talking.

When we girls in the band drove to work at night, we caught the attention of all the young kids in the neighborhood. They would crowd around our cars and reach in through the windows just to touch us. Maybe they thought we were famous. I remember one little girl touching

Hilda's hair and telling her how beautiful it was. Hilda was a bit taken aback but she was very sweet and thanked the little girl.

In our formal gowns and our stage makeup we probably did look like celebrities. But of course, at the time, I couldn't understand what all the fuss was about. It was a good gig, the crowds were great, and we were received very well, but when the week was finished we were glad to move on to a more comfortable situation away from the heat of that dim-lit city.

St. Louis, Missouri

WE LEARNED SOME DIFFICULT LESSONS IN ST. LOUIS. WHEN we got off our train for the first time, and were standing around our luggage waiting for cabs, we noticed another band standing nearby. We just naturally started talking.

Gradually we became aware that everyone around us was acting nervous and we realized that what we had done was a no-no in the South. Here was an all-girl, all-white band talking to an all-male, all-black band. People were staring at us so we rather awkwardly moved on. I just could not imagine not admiring the black musicians.

We lived at the Kingsway Hotel, a gracious old hotel on a major artery of the city. The hotel did not have air conditioning, but you felt a sort of coolness once you entered the lobby with its high ceilings and huge columns. The upholstered chairs and end tables and large potted plants lent the place an air of comfort. There was a courtyard outside where a few children played every day while their mothers sat in the shade and watched them. It seemed to be a nice family-type hotel. Hilda and I and two other girls were given a corner room with lots of windows, so we stayed fairly comfortable most of the time.

Since St. Louis was so incredibly hot we often took a bus to a swimming pool at the park. But it was hardly worth the effort because getting back on the bus put us back in the heat again. Hilda and I found more comfort visiting neighborhood shops. One afternoon a lady approached us and was excited because I was wearing one of "her" dresses. It was just a simple blue-and-white-striped seersucker fabric, but apparently it was from a line of clothes that had been designed for small dress shops and department stores. The compliment made me feel justified in shopping for even more dresses.

The dance hall was so hot and humid that not even huge fans helped to cool it much. It was an effort to play with enthusiasm, yet the crowds were good and the dancers didn't seem bothered by the heat.

One of the girls met a guy who wanted to take her out after work. He also wanted to fix his buddy up with me. But I hadn't met his buddy and I had a strict policy against blind dates. Too often, they were guys who just wanted to say they'd dated a girl in the band. I resented that.

This time, however, the blind date turned out to be a Native American. When I still wouldn't go out with him, his friend got mad and accused me of being racist. I could have gone out with him to keep peace, but it seemed more important to stick to my principles. I didn't go.

The old Kingsway Hotel was a charming place. Other guests were always friendly and chatted with us when we met them coming or going. The shopkeepers were the same — always welcomed us.

We had no reason to leave the neighborhood except to go to work. There were probably historical places to see but we chose to stay in our own little comfort zone until it was time to move on again.

Barksdale Field, Louisiana

Sweet swing with a distinctly feminine tone will be the musical treat in store for the Barksdale GI's Sunday evening when Freddie Shaffer brings his thirteen piece Victory Sweethearts dance band to the Hangar rostrum for a concert starting at 8:00 p.m.

The all-girl orchestra, currently playing a return engagement at the Coronado Club, are devoting a portion of their day off to come to the field to play for the service men here, and they will find themselves in a familiar atmosphere for they recently completed a swing around the USO circuit which took them to 327 different army and navy installations.

Jimmy Fiddler, Hollywood columnist, recently credited the band with presenting the best camp show that had come to his attention.

The group of talented girl musicians was organized five years ago in Indianapolis, Indiana, where Shaffer was music instructor in a group of twelve schools. A former orchestra man with experience in Paul Whiteman's and Isham Jones' bands, he carefully selected the girls for their musical ability and has been successful in keeping the original group intact with the exception of three girls.

—The *Barksdale Bark*, airbase newspaper, June 3, 1944

THE CORONADO CLUB WAS IN WHAT SEEMED A REMOTE AREA near the airbase, Barksdale Field, and was not far from Shreveport, Louisiana. We stayed in a motel next to the club and next to that was a restaurant. During the day there was absolutely nothing to do and it was unbearably hot. In those days, the motels didn't have big neon signs announcing swimming pools and Sunday brunch — kids eat or sleep free. If we wanted to do something we had to get on a bus and go into Shreveport or the smaller towns nearby.

Freddie came up with an idea to relieve us of our boredom. He decided this was an opportunity for the band to improve so he put us to work and got us out of the heat. After breakfast we met at the club for day one of many very intense music lessons. Freddie said that we needed to start over — learn the basics so to speak. We started by relearning the scales and chords in every key. We individually had to stand up in front of everyone to deliver our lessons. If we made a mistake, we were fined a dollar. In the back of all our minds was how quickly those dollars could add up. Yet we made few mistakes and it wasn't long before we rather enjoyed the contest.

Whether we liked it or not, it was a good idea. The afternoons were easy because all we had to do then was rehearse new songs and prepare a radio broadcast for that evening.

The club was packed every night and, of course, a lot of our audience was from Barksdale Field. Our most loyal fans were a group of flyers who came in every night after flight training to report on how the broadcast sounded from "up there." It was a thrill to have the attention of these handsome men in uniform and to be admired for what we were doing to entertain them. It's no wonder that I acquired a huge crush on a certain dark-haired, blue-eyed lieutenant. And I wasn't the only one in the band to be smitten by these most charming and handsome flyers.

Sundays were the only days we had free to do whatever we wanted. It was then that some of us were invited to come to Barksdale Field to join our dates at the officers' club for drinks and conversation. We dressed in our Sunday best and took a bus to the field. It was very nice being treated like royalty. I had no idea at that time that officers enjoyed many privileges denied to the GI's. The officers had a swimming pool we were invited to use a few times late at night. This was my first experience with the military. I had missed the long USO tour and wasn't quite aware of protocol. But gradually I became aware of the distance between the officers and the non-commissioned men.

As much as we liked some of the officers, we held to our own game plan when it came to handling any men: Never be alone with them. After work we always went someplace to eat a late dinner. In Barksdale it was the restaurant next door. Most guys didn't have a problem with our dating policy, but I remember one night we piled into the restaurant to find Hilda alone with her date. She motioned us to come over and join their table. This did not please her friend. He made some sarcastic remark like, "Why don't you invite all your relatives while you're at it?" Too bad, but that's the way it was, and we didn't often break that rule for anyone.

One Sunday afternoon we were asked to play for the enlisted men in a huge aircraft hangar, the largest building I had ever been in. The acoustics were terrible but it didn't matter to the GI's. They cheered, hollered, whistled, and applauded. The excitement was so intense and emotional that at times I was close to tears. I couldn't believe that what I was doing could affect so many people this way. When Hilda or Arthella sang, the men went wild. Hilda usually sang the bouncy songs like "Don't Sit Under the Apple Tree with Anyone Else but Me." And Arthella sang mostly ballads, like "I Love You for Sentimental Reasons." We had every popular tune of the day in our library.

When the concert was over an officer made a few announcements and then everyone was ordered back to their quarters and dismissed. We packed up and were on our way back to the club in short order. There we unpacked the instruments, changed clothes, and had a bite to eat. Then we went to our rooms to spend the rest of the evening doing what girls did — washing our hair, writing letters, or just having quiet time until it was time for sleep. We had to be fresh for the next day when the whole process started again.

The second time we played the Coronado Club was just as much fun as the first except that the lieutenant I had dated before had been shipped overseas. He sent a friend of his to introduce himself to me and explain why my lieutenant was not there anymore. In time the friend asked me to go out with him and I did. He was very nice and I liked him a lot. When the band finished and we were ready to move on, he gave me his address and I gave him my address and a small picture of myself. We wrote to each other for a while. Then the letters stopped. I found out later that after he was shipped out he ended up at the same base as his friend. At some point they got together and showed off pictures of their girlfriends. Both pictures were of me.

Edna, Shreveport, 1943

The Aragon Ballroom
Cleveland, Ohio

Gene Wolff, Detroit, 1940

WE DROVE INTO CLEVELAND IN OUR BIG OLD BLACK BUICKS
and the Woody station wagon and cruised slowly down Euclid Avenue
looking for our hotel. Cleveland was the largest city I had ever been in.
While I had been back in high school the rest of the band had been
booked to play in a lot of big cities, but I had missed out on it.

We arrived a day early, so after we were settled in and had had
dinner, some of us went to the Aragon Ballroom to hear the Clooney sisters with Tony Pastore's band. We would be on this same stage the next
night. I think we were the mid-week band and the weekends were
reserved for the big-name bands. The Aragon was a popular dance hall
and was packed with dancers every night. Hundreds of others lined the
stage just watching the musicians. I could never figure out what they were
looking for. You would often see someone whisper to the person next to
him and point to one of the musicians. It was intimidating wondering

what they were discussing. Could they tell if we were out of tune or flubbed a note? Or did they just think they knew everything about dance bands? Every night they were there. I wanted them to go dance, go have fun — but to stop watching me.

Another band, Bob Chester's, was booked to play at one of the big ballrooms in town, but they were staying in our hotel. It wasn't long before they were checking us out, curious about this all-girl dance band they had heard about. After our first night at the Aragon, we came back to our hotel to change clothes and go across the street to an all-night restaurant for something to eat. Right behind us came members of Chester's band. They started a conversation by asking who played trumpet, who played drums, who played trombone. When they asked who played sax I held up my hand and a tall man came over and introduced himself. His name was Gene and he too played sax. Some of the guys stood around our table and talked while others sat on stools at the bar. We talked for quite a while. Gene and I chatted along with the others, until we girls finally excused ourselves and went back to the hotel.

It was nice being able to talk to guys we had something in common with. We started seeing them more often. They must have waited for us in the lobby because they were always there, eager to talk, when we came down to go out. One night after work one of the guys invited us up to his room to listen to jazz on his record player. Gene was there, and paid more attention to me. I was attracted to him but was trying to be cool about it.

We had the weekend off because another big band was coming in. Gene called and asked if I would like to go to a movie and for a drink afterward. I said fine. The movie turned out to be *It's a Wonderful Life*. It had just come out in 1946 and was a big hit. After the movie I suggested a little bar nearby that some of our band had gone to several times because it had a good jazz group. We went. Gene raised an eyebrow when all the guys in the combo knew me by my first name. We sat in a booth and talked for hours and after we walked back to the hotel we sat in the lobby and talked until the early hours of the morning. Gene told me about being in Chester's band and I told him about being in Freddie's. It turned out we'd had a lot of similar experiences.

What impressed me most was that Gene didn't want to stay on the road. He planned to quit soon and go back to Michigan State University to finish his civil engineering degree. I had been on the road too long by then and was not interested in getting serious with a musician. Living in buses and hotels was a hard life for married couples. Gene's plans for the future seemed carefully thought out. I liked that. But the next morning, early, he called to say goodbye. His band was leaving on the road again. He said he would keep in touch.

Keep in touch he did — almost every other day. On Valentine's day I received a giant box of candy. The girls were impressed. I was too. Our bands were on the same circuit so Gene started leaving notes for me at box offices and hotel desks. I did the same and once left a tie as a present for his birthday. Once, Gene visited me while my band was playing in Morgantown, West Virginia, and he confessed that he'd hocked his clarinet to get enough money to travel there and back. He couldn't afford a room so once again we sat up all night together, this time on the balcony of Morgantown's old hotel. He talked more about his plans for the future and I was pleased to hear that he still intended to quit the music business. By then I'd seen what a hardship it was for band wives to travel and just sit and wait night after night. The money we earned was sufficient for single people, but wasn't enough for married couples.

Early in the morning our conversation was interrupted by a steady stream of hotel guests going to the bathroom to shower and get ready for their day. We got some strange stares from people who were still in their night clothes, carrying towels and toothbrushes. It felt like we were intruding in their home.

It was daylight by then, and again Gene had to take off to join his band. There had been a lot of flooding in the area so he caught a bus right outside the hotel instead of at the bus station, which was under water.

During the next few months we played mostly one-nighters. Finally I had a weekend off, so Gene asked me to come to Detroit to meet his family. I was nervous, of course, but they seemed to like me and made sure I felt welcome. His mother was terribly crippled with arthritis but the family seemed very happy. His father was a big teaser and loved to joke around. Pretty corny sometimes, but funny. His sister lived at home also. They had a rather small house so I stayed with family friends down the street. I remember being gently awakened in the morning with a tray of orange juice, toast, and coffee. Lovely people. Gene picked me up and took me back to his house where we visited with his mother. She ate her breakfast in the dining room with her pet parakeet perched on one finger. She shared her toast with the bird. I thought it kind of cute although I never would have thought of a bird as my best breakfast buddy.

Gene had apparently already told his mother that this was the girl he was going to marry. They had decided that I was to have her engagement ring, which she had not been able to wear for many years. After Gene and I left she packaged it up with a box of socks and sent it to him in care of me. This was back in Akron, where Freddie and the girls and I were booked for a stint and Gene's band was playing one-nighters. When I received the box, I didn't pay much attention to the way it was addressed and went ahead and opened it. The first thing I saw was a little black ring box and a letter from Gene's mother explaining that this was the ring I was to have. It was a lovely old-style ring, very ornate with white and yellow gold and an impressive stone. And it fit perfectly. The next time Gene called I laughed nervously and said, "Guess what? We're engaged."

He wasn't upset that I'd spoiled the surprise; in fact he seemed really pleased. By then we had already discovered that we never did things the way other people did. I loved the ring, but I was not yet ready for marriage.

About that time Freddie booked us to go on tour with Mischa Auer and Bonnie Baker. Mischa Auer was billed as a "mad Russian" comedian of the type seen in the movies. Bonnie Baker was popular because of her song "Oh, Johnny, Oh!", which she sang in a small, child-like voice. She was billed as Wee Bonnie Baker. With them was another singer, named Allegra.

It was a very funny and entertaining show. We performed four shows a day at local movie theaters. Sometimes, especially for the 4:30 show, almost no audience would show up at all. That's when things got really crazy. Mischa Auer would sit on the edge of the stage and joke with the few people in the audience. Those of us in the band would laugh so hard that we would miss our cues and not be able to read our music. Gene had a couple of days off, and since he had nothing else to do would sit

through all four shows. Often he was the only person in the audience. It was amazing to watch everyone perform their entire act to a nearly empty theater. This is what's meant by "the show must go on."

Gene was getting serious about marriage but I still wasn't ready. The music business was changing and I was getting tired of being on the road all the time, but I couldn't quite bring myself to leave that life. Gene came to Marion, Ohio, while we were on tour with the Mischa Auer and Bonnie Baker show. By now he had asked me nine times to marry him. Now he said he would not ask again: If I wanted to get married, it was up to me to say so. I thought it over for a few hours before deciding, yes, I was ready.

While the girls and I played our afternoon shows, Gene found a city office where we could get a blood test and marriage license. So between shows we went to an ancient upstairs office and waited our turn in line. I had my stage makeup on and judging from the stares I received, people must have gotten the wrong idea. I probably looked more like a hooker than a musician. But we left that office with our blood tested and our marriage licensed. Now all we had to do was go through the ceremony.

According to the law, we had to get married within thirty days or do the whole thing over again. And we had to do it in Ohio. I had one day off in the next month — May 27th — and Gene was playing in Toledo that night. His mother called me to ask if I was serious because if I was, she and Gene's father were ready to come to Toledo and be part of our wedding. I told her that we were ready. This was it. I hopped a bus to Toledo and his folks drove down from Detroit.

I had called my parents to tell them the news. I wanted them to come if they could, and since my father was a railroad man, they could have ridden the train at no cost at all. But mother was not feeling well — she was having another of her spells — and in the end they decided not to come.

I knew Mom would want us to be married in a church, so Gene and I found a Methodist Church and a wonderful minister who agreed to marry us on the spot, perhaps because with Gene's parents present he knew we were serious. The minister did everything he could to make it special. He stepped on a button on the floor and, presto, we had beautiful music for our ceremony. It was short but very nice. Gene's parents took us to dinner and then they left for Detroit and Gene and I hurried to his gig. While he played I sat in a corner by myself and watched. Bob Chester announced to the audience that one of his band members had just gotten married. I was a little embarrassed but happy at the same time. It seemed like an adventure out of a romantic movie.

I was to be in Hamilton, Ohio, the next day to continue our tour with Mischa Auer and Bonnie Baker. A train was scheduled to leave Toledo at 11:30 that night but Gene was supposed to play until 12:00. Bob Chester let him off early so we could make our train. We boarded on time, but then sat there for several hours without moving. The train had broken down in the station.

We were late getting into Hamilton and by the time we checked into our hotel, no rooms were available. The desk clerk said that even Mischa Auer was sleeping in the dining room on a cot. The day clerk came on duty and offered to have his room cleaned so that we could get some sleep there. We were dead tired and I had cramps. Some honeymoon. But we were finally together and at least were able to be close for a few hours of sleep before I had to be at the theater for the first show.

After our brief rest, we went to a little Italian restaurant for our first meal together as a married couple and then Gene had to catch a flight out so he could be in Buffalo where Chester's band was playing at a hotel that night. Then, at the airport, everything fell apart. There had been tornadoes throughout the Midwest and all flights had been canceled. Gene finally found a cab driver who agreed to drive him to Buffalo. It was the ride of Gene's life. Trees were down, roads closed, and still more bad weather was sweeping through the area. They finally reached Buffalo and Gene walked on stage a half hour late. Bob Chester immediately fired him. The band manager tried to intervene but Chester was adamant. He would allow Gene to play for two more weeks, but then he was out.

That settled it for Gene. He didn't want to try to join another band. Instead, he returned home to Detroit, determined to get a job or go back to college. He found a good job as a draftsman and moved in with his parents to wait for his bride to come home.

Leaving the band was not easy. It had been my life for so long and I just couldn't leave before Freddie found a replacement to play my part. And, of course, girl saxophone players were rare. I ended up returning with the band to Geneva-on-the-Lake and played there the whole summer. One night a policeman came to the bandstand and asked for me. I was more than a little surprised: What did he want with me? Well, this quaint little resort had only one pay phone, which was located at the other end of the village, and Gene had called the resort trying to reach me, and the policeman took the call, and somehow he found me, and he walked me to the phone. Gene was insistent: It was time I quit the band.

Soon afterward, Freddie found my replacement, a girl from back home in Frankfort. She wasn't quite ready for the job, so I stayed with the band the rest of the summer season until she was familiar with our repertoire. After Labor Day, when the resort closed, on September 9, 1947, I was finally on a bus to Detroit to live with my husband. I was ready to start living like a normal married person. I was ready for a home and a family and dinner on the table every evening at 6:00 when my husband came home from work.

Now all I had to do was learn how to cook.

Epilogue
The Morning After

MARRIED LIFE WAS EVERYTHING I HAD HOPED IT WOULD BE. I loved being in a real home and sending my husband off to work every day and spending our evenings with his friends talking about how car-crazy they were in their younger years. I liked Gene's friends and their wives, but I contributed little to the conversations. My career as a musician meant nothing to them.

In time I lost track of most of the girls in the band. I heard through the grapevine that they started dropping out because the band stopped being fun. The word was that Freddie was drinking more, which must have made it harder to get along with him. Lois quit to form her own band, and others quit to get married. Edna dropped out to be with her husband and have babies, but when her kids were three and four years old, Freddie talked her into returning occasionally to fill in with the band, sometimes offering to pay her babysitter in order to lure her to a

One of Edna's last jobs on the road with the band, Crystal, Michigan, 1951

gig. Hilda quit the band and returned to Frankfort, where she met Al and got married.

The band's last gig was in 1953 at the Indiana Roof. Edna played that last show; she and Arthella were the only ones left from the original band.

After the band dissolved, Freddie bought a grocery store near his home in Frankfort. Sometime later he got pneumonia, but stubbornly refused medical attention. By the time he consented to treatment it was too late. He died shortly after entering the hospital.

After I left the band I needed a job but discovered that I was spectacularly unqualified for almost anything. While we were staying with Gene's parents, I decided I could at least be a receptionist. I was used to being around people and, with the fortune I had spent on clothes, could make a good appearance. I got an appointment with the head of personnel at Ford Motor Company. I thought the interview went quite well. I had no problem talking with this man. He was friendly and charming and seemed interested in my work and the fact that I had been on my own in the band for so long. I confessed that I didn't know how to type, or take dictation, had never done any filing, and couldn't run a switchboard — was untrained in any of the usual jobs available to women in those days. (I didn't mention all the pants pockets I made back in Indiana during those two days at Levi Strauss.) Finally the man sat back in his big leather chair and said, "Mrs. Wolff, don't you know how to do anything?" I was stunned. He very politely showed me to the door and that was that. There wasn't even the hollow promise of a call if anything should open up.

I tried to find work as a musician but there were no big bands in the Detroit area and no work available for female sax players. Then we moved to Lansing so Gene could finish college and get his degree in civil engineering, and I finally got a job in a little dress shop. I was completely at ease showing clothes to women. Those many shopping sprees with Hilda had made me something of an expert.

But I had a goal to pursue, one that had been lurking in the back of my mind for years. In Lansing, Gene helped pay the bills by playing in a college dance band. One weekend they were short of musicians and Gene told his bandleader that I could read their book. I was given the fourth tenor part and played all evening under the watchful eye of the bandleader. Later he told Gene that I hadn't made a single mistake. It was a great moment for me. Patsy the sax player, who wasn't bad for a woman, had finally played in an all-male band.

Then I put my horn away. The time came when we were buying a house and needed a little extra money, and I was able to get exactly what we needed by selling it.

Many adventures lay ahead — new homes in new cities in the five years before we had children, then careers for my husband and me — but my days as a professional musician were over. I never looked back.

Yet to this day, whenever I hear the haunting strains of "Moonglow," I get goose bumps and a lump in my throat. It's the opening of the curtains that I remember, and the smiling faces of the girls, and the applause.